SOVEREIGNTY

SOVEREIGNTY
Moral and Historical Perspectives

James Turner Johnson

Georgetown University Press   Washington, DC

Library of Congress Cataloging-in-Publication Data

Johnson, James Turner.
Sovereignty : moral and historical perspectives / James Turner Johnson.
pages cm
Includes bibliographical references and index.
ISBN 978-1-62616-056-9 (pbk. : alk. paper)
1. Sovereignty—Social aspects. 2. Sovereignty—History. I. Title.
JC327.J55 2014
320.1'5—dc23

2013026133

∞ This book is printed on acid-free paper meeting the requirements of the American National Standard for Permanence in Paper for Printed Library Materials.

15 14 9 8 7 6 5 4 3 2 First printing
Printed in the United States of America

Contents

Introduction

The idea of sovereignty, in present-day usage, almost always has reference to the state and to the international system based on states, known alternatively as "the Westphalian system" or as "the United Nations system." The meaning of the latter is obvious; that of the former refers back to the Peace of Westphalia of 1648, a collection of international agreements that ended the Thirty Years' War. The modern state system is generally understood to be built on the terms of the Peace of Westphalia. The idea of sovereignty associated with the modern state and system of states is only a bit older, tracing to Hugo Grotius's widely influential *De iure belli ac pacis* (*On the Laws of War and Peace*), first published in 1625 but soon afterward available in a variety of translations and editions. The essentials of this conception of sovereignty were a particular national territory inhabited by a particular people with their particular history, expressed in the patterns of everyday life and in their laws, customs, and institutions, and the right of the people to defend all this against any challenge to it. In this understanding two characteristics stand out: the definition of sovereignty in terms of territory that may be defended and the concept of the people as having one fundamental right, that of self-defense, whose exercise they delegate, within the political community, to their rulers for defense of the entire national territory. All of this is today encapsulated in Article 2(4) of the United Nations Charter, which forbids the threat or use of force by one member state against "the territorial integrity or political independence" of another, and Article 51, which affirms the right of states to self-defense in case of such wrongful use of force. The conception of sovereignty in general use today thus traces to the seventeenth century, but it has endured into the present, with the language of the Charter echoing the thinking of Grotius and the system of states built on the Peace of Westphalia.

There is, though, an older conception of sovereignty that this modern one replaced, one that differs importantly from the modern one: a conception of sovereignty not in terms of the state and its territorial inviolability but in terms of the moral responsibility of the ruler for the common good of the people governed. This is the conception of sovereignty one encounters in the classic statements of the idea of just war and the tradition that came out of them, where the right to use force is limited to those temporal rulers with no temporal superiors, who are thus the persons having final responsibility, in their political communities, for ensuring that justice is protected and preserved, thereby establishing public peace. Here the right to use force is tied explicitly to the obligation to protect and preserve justice by restoring it when it has been violated and by punishing those persons responsible for the violation. The sovereign ruler, on this conception, has the obligation to establish an order in which justice is the norm, and thus to establish peace in his (or her or in some cases their) own domains and in relation to other political communities. Thus would the common good be served. The idea of sovereignty, understood in this way, had first reference to the person of the sovereign ruler and that person's responsibility for the common good of the political community ruled—and, by extension, the good of the larger community of all political communities, whose relations should also be characterized by justice in order that peace should hold sway among them.

This was the conception of sovereignty I encountered in my historical and analytical work on the tradition of just war. In its specific formulation and in the assumptions on which it rested, it was a Western conception, a product of Western cultural experience. But when I became interested in the Islamic tradition on jihad of the sword and its place in the government of the Islamic community and that community's relations with non-Muslim societies, I discovered a similar idea there, though framed in terms of reflections based on the Qur'an, the Hadith literature, and the Muslim community's experience with the world: a ruler whose right to rule rested on his (always his in this tradition) obligation to ensure justice in human affairs.

In investigating the tradition of just war, its origins and development, and its current use, as in investigating the tradition on jihad of the sword, its historical meaning and use, and the present-day adaptation of the idea of such jihad especially by radical Islamists like those of al-Qaeda, my concerns have mostly focused on the uses of armed force itself: who might use it, under what necessary justifications, to what end, and with what limits on how such force might be employed. But in the 1990s, in the context of the moral and political debates over humanitarian intervention occasioned by the wars over the breakup of Yugoslavia, the Rwandan massacre of 1994, and other conflicts from this period, I began to think in a more focused way about the matter of sovereignty itself. That the possibility of humanitarian intervention by force could be seriously debated at all in this context was the result of the collapse of the Soviet Union and the end of the Cold War: A use of armed force for humanitarian purposes in a politically sensitive part of the world could be contemplated without fearing that it might start a third World War. But that there should be such a debate at all rested on the broad international growth of concern over human rights and the development of international human rights law following the Universal Declaration on Human Rights of 1948: The debate over humanitarian intervention took shape as having to do with preventing, stopping, and remedying massive, systematic, continuing violations of basic human rights. Doing so might easily seem, from the perspective of human rights law taken by itself, an obviously good thing, but there was a problem with this conclusion: Existing international law, indeed the international system itself, rests on a conception of sovereignty in terms of the inviolability of national territory and the right of states to defend themselves against any use of armed force, for whatever reason, across their borders, and this law as written makes no exceptions for the protection of human rights.

In international law, besides the provisions of Articles 2(4) and 51 of the United Nations Charter noted above, another pairing of elements of the Charter extends the same ground rules to the United Nations as a body: Article 2(7) denies the right of the United Nations "to intervene in matters which are essentially within the domestic jurisdiction of any state," though Chapter VII, specifically in Articles 39, 41, and 42, gives the Security Council the right to undertake such intervention by force in cases of "any threat, breach of the peace, or act of aggression." Significantly, Article 51 is also a part of Chapter VII, so that while the Security Council has the right to use armed force, the state against which such force is used retains the right of self-defense. Even assuming that Article 2(4) rules out any state's projecting force across the borders of another even for humanitarian purposes, how a government treats its own populace looks very much to be a matter "within the domestic jurisdiction" of that state, so long as it is not a threat to international peace. The implications of human rights law, as well as moral motivations to protect basic human rights from violation, thus ran right up against the prohibitions in the Charter against the use of armed force across national borders. These latter prohibitions derive directly from the modern conception of sovereignty in terms of territorial inviolability of states and the correlated right of self-defense against any violation of a state's territorial borders. But thinking of the matter of humanitarian intervention in terms of just war tradition, I thought of sovereignty in a different way: as responsibility for the common good. The result was to encounter a dilemma similar to that encountered from the perspective of human rights law: Humanitarian intervention, from the just war perspective, might be a moral obligation; yet at the same time, it would be a violation of international law. The two conceptions of sovereignty and their implications were thus in direct conflict with each other. In important respects the current book represents my reflections toward resolving the dilemma this opposition poses.

This book examines the idea of sovereignty in its historical development, focusing on the moral dimensions of major ways of understanding this concept and the implications of how sovereignty is understood for the lives of political communities and the relations of such communities with one another. Sovereignty is a Western idea in its origins and much of its historical evolution, though the incorporation of a particular understanding of sovereignty into international law and its broad use throughout the international order argue for its universal relevance. In this book the focus of part I, which treats the two conceptions of sovereignty sketched above, how they developed, and their implications, is on Western thinking and experience, whereas part II turns to the case of Islamic thought and practice and then to the international debate over the idea of "the responsibility to protect." Most of the historical figures treated in part I are immediately recognizable as ecclesiastical lawyers and theologians; the historical figures who shaped the corresponding tradition on politics and government in Islamic tradition were likewise religious jurists. From a post-Enlightenment perspective, this connection to religion suggests that they could have nothing worth saying about political life, which is understood to belong to a different sphere. To the contrary, I would say first that these historical figures, Christian and Muslim, all understood the importance of thinking about questions of politics and government, including the conception of sovereignty, in terms of what is shared by all humanity: nature, not grace; natural law, not church morality; not Islam as a revelation given to a specific people but what is natural to all humankind. Second, when one reads in the thought of these people, one immediately encounters thinking in close dialogue with the realities of the temporal world and its responsibilities, including those of political life and government. It would be a major conceptual—and historical—mistake to disregard their thinking as irrelevant to the world of politics. It may well be that the specifically religious sensitivities of these thinkers led them to conceive sovereignty in terms of responsibility for the common good and not in the modern sense where this responsibility does not appear, but that, I suggest, is a gain relative to the modern conception.

Though the understanding of sovereignty as moral responsibility took shape in connection with the idea of just war, this understanding and its priority in classical just war thinking have been largely and often entirely absent from the main lines of recent just war thinking. Paul Ramsey, whose work in the 1960s consciously attempted to recover the idea of just war as an implication of the Christian obligation to love the neighbor, regarded the use of armed force as belonging to the tools of the proper exercise of statecraft, but the emphasis in his work was elsewhere, not on the use of force in the service of justice and the common good but on the restraints to be observed in the use of force (discrimination, or avoiding direct, intended harm to noncombatants, and proportionality, implying avoidance of excessive destructive power). Michael Walzer, to whose *Just and Unjust Wars* (1977) most subsequent philosophical thinking about just war directly or indirectly traces, casts the question of the use of armed force in terms of what he calls "the legalist paradigm," developing it under the rubric of "the theory of aggression." In other words, the frame used by Walzer is that of modern international law, where sovereignty is defined in terms of territorial integrity and the exercise of rule within such territory. When he treats the matter of responsibility in this book, it is in a separate section where the focus is not on the justified use of armed force but on the nature of the responsibilities political leaders and citizens have when war is unjust. Ramsey and Walzer are two of the main pillars of the recovery of discourse about just war in recent American debate.

The third pillar, which in effect completed that recovery because of the widespread attention it claimed, was the pastoral letter of the United States Catholic bishops, *The Challenge of Peace*, published in 1983. Catholic teaching on just war here was defined as beginning with a "presumption against war," with the idea of just war providing a series of requirements that, if all are met, can overturn this "presumption." In this statement the requirement of authority for war, described as "competent authority," is placed not first but second, with the need for just cause given priority. In terms of the logic of the argument, this implies that the decision as to just cause may be made by others than those responsible for government (the bishops themselves, perhaps?), and that the role of the "competent authority" is dependent on that judgment and is not to weigh the issues and determine justice or injustice as essential to the exercise of such authority. Though the requirement of "competent authority" to use force is described as "joined to the common good" and as limiting the use of force to "those with responsibility for public order," this requirement, in the bishops' conception, is a secondary one, not primary, and the idea of responsibility is not explored or developed.

To understand the emphasis on sovereignty and its definition in terms of responsibility for the common good, one thus has to move beyond such conceptions of just war as these and subsequent contemporary just war thinking that defines the idea of just war differently from the classical tradition. These present-day conceptions, in focusing on war-conduct or proceeding from the assumptions built into the present-day international order, entirely miss the critical moral significance attaching to the conception of sovereignty and its importance in historical just war thinking. The investigation undertaken in this book, then, has to do not only with the idea of sovereignty and its development but also with understanding the core of the idea of just war in its historical expression and development.

I do not, though, intend this book simply as an exercise in the retrieval of ideas from the past; rather, as part II especially shows, I mean it to provide a contribution to the ongoing debate of the last two decades over government, states, the international order, and the responsibilities of each. So far as this debate has proceeded solely on the idea of sovereignty embedded in the Westphalian–United Nations system, it has not taken account of the deeper tradition in Western culture and the corresponding traditions in other major cultures that understand government, the political community, and the interrelations among such communities in terms of deep moral values. This book aims not only to recall those values but to place reflection based on them into the ongoing debate.

I

Sovereign Authority and the Right to Use Armed Force in Classic Just War Tradition

1

Sovereignty as Responsibility

The Coming Together and Development of a Tradition

While the origins of the idea of sovereignty as responsibility for the common good of the political community can be traced further back in history, the coming together of the specific tradition on this idea that is the focus of this book traces to the same beginnings as the just war tradition: the medieval intellectual revival of the late twelfth and thirteenth centuries. The traditions on just war and sovereignty as responsibility are intimately mixed together and ultimately inseparable: They began together and subsequently developed together. They are not identical, since just war tradition has to do with one specific element in understanding the implications of the understanding of sovereignty as responsibility for the common good, namely, the sovereign's use of armed force in the discharge of that responsibility. But one learns a great deal about the understanding of just war from the perspective of the inner meaning and practical implications of this conception of sovereignty, and vice versa, one may learn a great deal about the inner meaning and practical implications of this understanding of sovereignty from how it is laid out in connection with the question of just war, *bellum iustum*.

The conceptualization of both sovereignty and just war during this period took place in a rich intellectual context shaped by two major influences: the Augustinian heritage and the recovery of Roman traditions on natural law, the associated concept of rights, and *ius gentium*. Similarly, the changed shape of thinking about both just war and sovereignty that appeared early in the modern age reflected changes in how these two elements in the earlier cultural and intellectual context were interpreted and understood to apply. This chapter examines these two influences as they bore on the ideas of sovereignty as responsibility and just war in their coming together and development as moral and political traditions.

The Augustinian Heritage, the Idea of Just War, and the Idea of Sovereignty

When exploring core ideas about the nature, goals, and obligations of political life in Western culture, one runs up against the influence of Augustine at virtually every turn. It is difficult to overstate the impact of his thought on these core ideas and thus on the theoretical structures and institutions later developed to express them. Not only early Christian theology but assumptions about classical culture and representations of it were funneled and filtered by Augustine's thought, expressed through his writings, into the Middle Ages, on to the theologians and political theorists of the early modern period, and through their influence on to later generations. So fundamental was Augustine's thought in the Middle Ages that even when new influences arose, as illustrated by the recovery of Aristotle in the thirteenth century and by the broader recovery of classical culture in the Renaissance, the new thinking that grew out of these influences also reflected Augustinian conceptions. Concern for Augustine's thought in the present book focuses on his influence on the ideas of just war and of the good ruler, which define and express a conception of sovereignty in the political order as fundamentally moral.

Augustine has frequently been characterized as the originator of the just war idea and the first just war theologian. These characterizations reflect and honor the depth of his influence on Western culture generally and on Christian thought in particular, but they are true only up to a point. As to his place in the history of just war thinking, a close look at what he wrote about just war shows that Augustine in framing his own position drew heavily on an established tradition of just war in Roman thought and practice, a tradition also related to earlier classical ideas and practice, as well as on conceptions of justified war from the Hebrew scriptures.[1] His conception of the requirements for a justified resort to armed force—the authority of a ruler, a just cause, and the intention of restoring or newly establishing peace—clearly reflected Roman thinking and practice. Augustine did not originate the just war idea; he built on traditions already existing. Nor did he produce a unified, well-developed, and systematic conception of just war; doing so was the work of medieval thinkers beginning with the canonist Gratian in the mid-twelfth century. By contrast to what he had to say about another moral subject, sexuality and marriage, which he treated extensively and systematically in several distinct theological treatises, what Augustine wrote about just war consists of a relatively small number of passages, typically brief, scattered through works of diverse sorts—letters, theological treatises, biblical commentary. These are the passages lifted out, collected, systematically organized, and oriented to practical reflection, decision making, and behavior by Gratian and then used by the canonists who succeeded him and by theologians like Thomas Aquinas and his successors. But the story consists of more than the specific passages cited from Augustine; it also includes the broader context of Augustine's own thought, especially as this was appropriated, assumed, and used by the medieval thinkers who organized and defined the idea of just war. For though Augustine built on late classical Roman ideas on just war, he did not simply restate them but put his own stamp on them as he employed them. For their part, his medieval successors also placed their stamp on the inheritance from Augustine by how they interpreted and used it.

To begin to penetrate and understand this Augustinian world, we may usefully consider the following quotations, several from Augustine, one from Isidore of Seville, and one from Paul's Epistle to the Romans.

First, from Augustine: "On the contrary, they were told: 'Do violence to no man; . . . and be content with your pay.' If he commanded them to be content with their pay, he did not forbid soldiering."[2]

Again from Augustine: "The natural order conducive to peace among mortals demands that the power to declare and counsel war should be in the hands of those who hold the supreme authority."[3]

And: "A just war is . . . one that avenges wrongs, when a nation or state has to be punished, for refusing to make amends for the wrongs inflicted by its subjects, or to restore what it has seized unjustly."[4]

From Isidore: "A war is just when . . . it is waged in order to regain what has been stolen or to repel the attack of enemies."[5]

Returning to Augustine: "What is it about war that is to be blamed? Is it that those who will die someday are killed so that those who will conquer might dominate in peace? This is the complaint of the timid, not of the religious. The desire for harming, the cruelty of revenge, the restless and implacable mind, the savageness of revolting, the lust for dominating, and similar things—these are what are justly blamed in wars."[6]

And this: "We do not seek peace in order to be at war, but we go to war that we may have peace. Be peaceful, therefore, in warring, so that you may vanquish those whom you war against, and bring them to the prosperity of peace."[7]

Finally, from the Book of Romans: "For rulers are not a terror to good conduct, but to bad. Would you have no fear of him who is in authority? Then do what is good, and you will receive his approval, for he is God's servant for your good. But if you do wrong, be afraid, for he does not bear the sword in vain; he is the servant of God to execute his wrath on the wrongdoer."[8]

These few passages constitute the core of the idea of just war as it first came together in Christian moral thought in the Middle Ages. All of them appear in the discussion of war in Gratian's *Decretum*; most appear also in Aquinas's question "On War." The first passage refutes the argument that Christians ought to reject all forms of the use of force but affirms that they may without sin serve in the armed forces of the political community. The second passage defines and restricts the right to resort to force to the "supreme authority" in that community, implicitly denying it to everyone else who would employ force on his own behalf, that is, anyone who would, in the language of the first passage, "do violence" to another, a distinction too often lost in present-day just war argumentation, but one central to the concept of just war in Augustine and in the Middle Ages, and one bearing directly on the question of the meaning of sovereignty as understood there.

The third and fourth passages clarify the limited range of causes that justify resort to force: for Augustine, punishing wrongdoing and restoring that which has been unjustly taken away; for Isidore, retaking that which has been stolen and defending against unjust attack. Gratian, who employed both of these quotations to define the category of just cause for resort to force, thus recognized three such causes, while Augustine (and Aquinas, who quoted only the passage from Augustine on this) did not explicitly mention defense against attack. Other causes that some might wish to include as justifications for resort to force are also absent here; these are passages that strictly limit what the sovereign (or "supreme") authority should look for.

In the fifth passage quoted, Augustine defines a number of kinds of intentions that are to be avoided in the use of force. For him the issue in the passage cited is one of inner attitude, mindset, or motivation toward the use of force itself and toward those against whom it is to be used. One does not use force justly if he is seduced by the power it gives him, if he uses it for his private interest or pleasure, or if he uses it out of blinding hatred for the enemy. This passage complements the next one quoted, which defines right intention in terms of its end: aiming to secure peace. This last passage from Augustine defines the ultimate purpose toward which all moral uses of force should aim: the restoration of peace where there has been war and the creation of peace where there has been none, along with a caution that one must fight "peacefully," that is, in a way that does not undermine the achievement of peace but rather supports it. As Augustine explicitly signals in the language he uses in the list of evil intentions in the passage from *Contra Faustum*, such evil intentions arise from sinful *cupiditas*, "self-love," and sinful *libido*, "lust," while the intention of securing peace, a good for all, is in accord with *caritas*, "charity," the kind of love that is directed toward the good of the neighbor, the triumph of the heavenly city, and life in the presence of God. Together these two passages define what both Augustine and his medieval successors who consolidated and systematized the idea of just war understood as the requirement of right intention. In their thinking, this requirement reinforced the condition that only persons in supreme or sovereign authority within a political community may justly engage in the use of force, for they bear the responsibility of aiming at the good of all, and in principle only the use of force under their authority can have this purpose, while the use of force by private persons is always inevitably tainted by *cupiditas*. But at the same time, Augustine's list of wrong intentions set limits on sovereigns, reminding them that they may not justly employ force out of such private reasons either.

Romans 13:3–4, the final passage quoted, stands as a kind of motto for medieval and early modern Christian thinking about the just use of force: The use of force belongs properly to the role of political authority as an element in God's government of the world. In the immediate context of the passages I have quoted from Augustine, it provides a weighty biblical source for why force should be morally restricted to the highest authority in the political community. Among medieval and early modern just war theorists, this is the main use to which this passage from Romans was put. But the passage also had another kind of influence: If the ruler is the servant of God who is to act in the stead of God to punish evildoing, some thinkers reasoned, then this shows what the ruler himself must be and what ought to be the quality of his rule and of the society he governs. Thus Romans 13:3–4 also became a foundational passage for a tradition of reflection on the good ruler and the good state, a tradition that helped to influence modern political theory on what good government should be and what aims should guide it. This tradition is examined further below.

Taken all together, then, these sparse passages I have quoted have had a great influence on Western thought on the use of force within the context of the political community and, from the perspective of the question of the justified use of force, on the conception of good government and the nature of the good political community itself. These passages first appeared in close, thematic connection with other passages from the Bible, from Augustine, and from other magisterial Christian theologians in the canonist Gratian's *Decretum* from the middle of the twelfth century. Their purpose there, and the purpose of canon law generally, was to guide Christian moral behavior by specifying right and wrong uses of force by Christians in the context of God's overall government of the world. The next two generations of canonists after Gratian, known as the Decretists and the Decretalists, respectively, focused mostly on the question of the use of force by the governing authority and on limiting the number or kinds of people who could claim a right to have recourse to arms. A century and a quarter after Gratian, the passages from Augustine and from Romans became the backbone of Thomas Aquinas's discussion of just war in the *Summa Theologiae*, where they were tied especially to the concept of responsibility in good government as exercised by the just ruler.

The Recovery and Redefinition of the Idea of Natural Law

In the twelfth century, the Roman conception of law was recovered, but this took place in a context deeply shaped by Augustinian ways of thinking. To examine the recovery and redefinition of the idea of natural law and associated concepts in this period, then, we need first to reflect on how Augustine had dealt with such law in his own work, for Augustine's influence loomed large over the medieval understanding of natural law. Yet Augustine's own thinking on this matter changed over his lifetime.

Commenting on Augustine's early treatise *De Libero Arbitrio*, R. A. Markus writes, "The just war, among other things, had been deeply embedded in the universal order, and Augustine's reflection on it was closely linked with his own theory of the eternal and the temporal law:

the soldier in killing has been a *minister legis* [*De Libero Arbitrio* I.5.12], executing a law which was itself distinct from but dependent on a *lex aeterna*."[9] Markus goes on to note that Augustine held to the core concepts identified here throughout his life, though he revised his thinking on law twice after this.[10] First was his new understanding of law in *Contra Faustum*, again offered in the context of a discussion of war (indeed, in the context of the longest specific discussion of just war found in his works). Here, influenced by the Theodosian regime's embrace of the Church, Augustine envisioned a state of affairs in which the law of the state was being increasingly conformed to the law of Christ, and the use of force by the state was an important element in bringing this to pass.

The second shift took place after *Contra Faustum*, in the last decades of Augustine's life. *The City of God*, written during this period, offers a more chastened view of the possibilities of the Roman state, which had been progressively diminished internally by the policies of emperors after Theodosius and beset by the military successes of the Visigoths in Italy, the fall of Rome to a Visigoth army in 410, and the later Vandal siege of Augustine's own city of Hippo Regius in North Africa. Early in *The City of God*, commenting on Cicero, Augustine notes that the Roman republic held in such high esteem by Cicero was imperfect by Cicero's own standard, since its justice was lacking in that in it God was not given his due,[11] and toward the end of the work he criticizes the Roman *tranquillitas ordinis*—the tranquility of everyday life that the order provided by Rome makes possible—as inferior to the final rest found in the City of God.[12] Nonetheless, Augustine in various contexts throughout this work makes a point of defending the order, justice, and peace that Rome, as the highest historical expression of the possibilities of the earthly city, has brought to its own people as well as to those it has conquered and subjugated.[13] The role of just war as Augustine sets it out here is not to fulfill divine prophecy, as it was sometimes described to be in *Contra Faustum*; it is instead to be an expression of political order to preserve as far as possible the goods necessary for human life and to protect them against disintegration and chaos. Involvement in this task is a moral obligation. Markus stresses this by citing the case of the judge discussed by Augustine in *The City of God* XXII.xxii: "'Will a wise man sit as judge in this darkness of social life (*in his tenebris vitae socialis*),' Augustine asks, 'or will he not dare? Of course he will sit, . . . for the solidarity of human society lays upon him this duty, and he would think it wrong to shirk it.'" The quest for justice and order is doomed; but dedication to the impossible task is demanded by the very precariousness of civilized order in the world.[14] Similarly, George Weigel (in a chapter titled "The Catholic Tradition of Moderate Realism") offers these observations:

> [Order] was the condition for the possibility of virtue in public life. The peace of this world was but "the peace of Babylon"; but such a peace was not to be deprecated: it allowed fallen human beings to "live and work together and attain the objects that are necessary for their earthly existence." Moreover, earthly peace makes an important contribution to the well-being and progress of those called to heavenly peace. . . . In this fallen world, war was inevitable. Like the authority of the state, war exists in God's providential plan as an instrument for punishment, so that a minimum of justice—that is, order—may be maintained.[15]

In the later stage of Augustine's life, the idea of a natural law defining the goods of human community—order, justice, and peace—is still visible but not as a perfection able to be embodied by any empirical human community. Yet even in *The City of God* these are presented as real goods, worthy of service and sacrifice, though they also appear as a kind of floor below which any earthly city dare not fall. There remain also those chapters elsewhere in the work in which Augustine gives credit to Rome for the benefits its rule has brought to those societies it has added to itself. Whatever the prospects of their achievement, these naturally defined goods remain the goals of political society, and in Augustine's conception, just war not only exists to serve these goods but is defined in terms of them: the good of order reflected in the requirement that there must be public authority for any resort to force; the good of justice reflected in Augustine's conception of just cause as for the recovery of things wrongly taken and the punishment of evildoing; and the good of peace reflected in Augustine's conception that just wars are instruments of peace.

When Augustine's scattered, topically occasioned, and diversely motivated discussions of just war were brought together and systematically arranged in the twelfth and thirteenth centuries, first by Gratian and his canonist successors and then by Aquinas in *Summa theologiae* II/II, Q. 40, A. 1, this linkage between the defining goods of political life and the requirements for just war was not only maintained but made more explicit, especially in Aquinas's pithy listing of the three requirements for a war to be just: the authority of a prince, a just cause, and a right intention, where the three requirements correspond directly to the defining political goods of order, justice, and peace.

But it is also important that this recovery and systematization took shape in a context in which the idea of natural law as treated in Roman thinking and practice apart from Augustine was also being recovered, systematized, and probed as to its meaning, and the same groups of people—first the canonists, then scholastic theologians—were responsible for both developments. These medieval thinkers were thus not dependent only on the idea of natural law as found in Augustine; rather, two other developments enriched their reflections. First, the entire corpus of Roman law was recovered during this same period, with a content that included not only Roman positive law but the ideas of *ius gentium* and *ius naturale*, and this corpus was being explored and analyzed by legal thinkers, canon and civil lawyers alike, as to its meaning and application to the medieval context. Second, though a bit later, knowledge of Aristotle's philosophy gained through Arabic sources, in particular Aristotle's understanding of natural law, was helping to shape new approaches in theology. In this rich soup of new inquiry and rediscovery of ancient ideas, the conception of natural law took on new dimensions. Brian Tierney comments: "Earlier the phrase *ius naturale* had been understood in an objective sense to mean natural law or 'what is naturally right.' But the canonists who wrote around 1200, reading the old texts in the context of their more humanist, more individualist culture, added another definition. In their writings, *ius naturale* was now defined in a subjective sense as a faculty, power, force, ability inhering in individual persons."[16] Tierney goes on to identify a number of rights deduced from this conception: ownership or property rights, the right of liberty, the right of forming governments, and the right of self-defense. The Roman idea of *ius gentium* was extended by this conception of rights, so that political communities were understood as independent entities with these same rights. Further, along with the rights came responsibilities and obligations, notably the responsibility of others to respect them and the obligation of rulers to protect the rights of their communities against threat or violation. When one reads Aquinas's magisterial summary of the three requirements for a just war, it is necessary to recognize, then, that he is not simply systematizing what Augustine had said, though he leans heavily on key Augustinian formulations, providing citations from Augustine on each of the three requirements he identifies; rather, he is adding content to those requirements in accord with the developments in thinking about *ius naturale* and *ius gentium* in the century before him.

Much of what the canonists and (later) the early Scholastics did aimed to achieve a synthesis among the disparate influences and perspectives with which they were working. Roman law, for the canonists, offered a persuasive model of such a synthesis, defining a normative relationship linking the positive law by which Rome governed to the laws and customs of particular peoples in the Empire (the *ius gentium*) and the underlying (or overarching) structure of the law of nature (*ius naturale*).

Of particular importance for thinking about both the use of arms and individual rights relative to the moral and political orders was the term *ius* (or *jus*, as often written and later printed), which, as already noted in the comment from Tierney above, developed new meanings in the process of its being recovered and interpreted in the twelfth and thirteenth centuries. The results were actually more complex than Tierney indicates. The Latin word *ius*, as employed in this period and beyond, carried three distinguishable and important meanings that expanded late classical Roman usage and that are normally distinguished from one another in English usage today: right, in the sense of proper or correct; right, in the sense of a claim one individual has in relation to another or to others; and law, not in the sense of *lex*, or positive law, but in the sense of the law that is "in one's members" or in nature, or the law expressed through expected customary behavior. These three meanings, distinguishable but not entirely distinct, remained in Latin usage through the rest of the Middle Ages and into the modern period. An example of the persistence of Latin usage in modern usage is provided by the title of Hugo Grotius's highly influential major work, *De iure belli ac pacis*, rendered into English as both *Of the Rights of War and Peace* and *Of the Laws of War and Peace*. Which is correct? The answer is both, for in the Latin both these meanings are carried by the same word, though in English they are distinguished.

The emergence of the subjective understanding of *ius*, so that it referred not only to what is right by the nature of things but also to a "right" possessed by individuals, was especially interesting. This in no way was taken to mean that everyone possessed all the same rights. For example, as regards the use of arms, every member of the knightly class in this period was understood to possess the right of arms, *ius armae*. This was a carryover from Germanic custom; people not of the knightly class had no such right. Nor, by canon law and church custom, did clerics and religious, whatever their social rank. For those to whom it applied, this was understood as an individual right: it was at once "right and proper," in the sense of being accepted as correct, and a reflection of the customary order of things. But the right to carry and employ arms in support of one's individual claims over others was not the same as the right of war (*ius bellare*), which referred to the right landed knights and higher nobles had to use arms for the good of the whole society encompassed by their landholdings. The right to war, *bellum*, referred specifically to the rights and responsibilities of a landed member of the knightly class to govern his lands and the people living on them, maintaining their personal security relative to one another, to the landowner himself, and to others from outside. Government on this conception was essentially judicial in function, with those in governing authority having the right of collective use of force (*bellum*) to maintain justice in the face of some fault. This is the meaning expressed in Gratian's citation of Isidore of Seville linking just war to the function of a judge.[17] Other uses of arms were not *bellum* but *duellum*, the settlement of private quarrels.

But the right to undertake *bellum* was not yet the right to undertake just war, *bellum iustum*. On this matter the canonists made an especially valuable distinction. When they defined the concept of just war, *bellum iustum*, they reserved this specific term for the use of arms by a temporal ruler with no temporal superior to correct and punish an injustice already accomplished with the aim of vindicating justice (*iustitia*, the right order of things) and thus ensuring the peace of the common order. The settled concept of *bellum iustum* thus depended on the right of arms, the *ius armae*, but limited it and channeled it to define the place of the use of armed force in the exercise of governing responsibility.

The Latin term employed for a temporal ruler with no temporal superior, one who alone had the right (*ius*) to wage *bellum iustum*, was *princeps*, "prince" (as for example in Aquinas's first condition for a just war, *auctoritas principis*, "princely authority" or "the authority of the prince"). In French and English the word *princeps* was contemporaneously replaced by *souverain*, "sovereign." The just war idea, as it came together in the late twelfth and thirteenth centuries, centered on a conception of sovereignty as responsibility for the common good of society that is to be exercised to vindicate justice after some injustice has occurred and gone unrectified or unpunished. This responsibility is fundamentally to and for the moral order itself, understood as an order in accord with the natural law, which itself was conceived as a manifestation of the divine will as embedded in the natural order. The responsibility of government on this conception is rather different from the present-day idea of "the responsibility to protect," where the responsibility is owed to groups of people by virtue of rights they are understood to possess as individuals simply by virtue of their humanity. This is a conception of rights that did not exist before the modern age or, indeed, before the work of such thinkers as Hobbes, Locke, and the eighteenth-century French philosophes.

The medieval and early modern conception of rights possessed by individuals did assume that these rights were grounded in custom or nature, but different individuals were understood as having different rights depending on social status, condition, age, and gender. Moreover, these rights were conceived as claims that particular individuals might make in relationship to others. People of higher social status were understood as having greater rights (that is, claims) over their social inferiors, not the other way around. But some rights, those understood as deeply rooted in nature or custom, entitled persons of socially inferior rank to make a claim against a social superior. Consider the original rationale for what we today call noncombatant immunity (a comparatively recent term). Both Church teaching and the chivalric code laid down that classes of persons who do not normally participate in war should not be directly, immediately attacked in *bellum*.[18] The rationale in each case proceeded from the moral order itself "downward" to the protection of the classes of noncombatants named in the various lists. For the churchly canons, they had committed no fault and thus it would be unjust to harm them; for the chivalric code, harming people who did not bear arms would bring dishonor on the knight who did so. Of course, the people in the protected classes were understood to have a "right" to be left alone, and in present-day usage this defines their immunity from harm; but in the frame of the thinking of the period, this "right" was a claim against those who might attack them, a claim that justified immediate self-defense against such attack or a subsequent claim for justice against the perpetrators. This is very different from saying that such a claim to be left alone defined their immunity from being attacked.

In any case, once harm had been accomplished, this was framed in the thinking of this period as a violation of justice that needed to be remedied, not a violation of rights. The focus was on the moral order itself, not on the individuals. Nor did their rights extend to seeking by their own powers to remedy the injustice done. This was rather the right—and the responsibility—of those in governing authority over those who had committed the fault. Again, sovereign responsibility in this frame was defined first of all in terms of responsibility to the moral order.

The synthesis that came out of the coincidence of the streams of rediscovery and new thinking I have been discussing cemented the locus of the right and responsibility to wage war within the temporal sphere, identified with the rights and responsibilities of temporal rulers with no temporal superiors, while leaving the Church supreme in spiritual matters. This distinction, which was unclear in pre-Christian Rome and which never developed robustly in Byzantine theory and practice, was understood in the medieval West by reference to the following statement from Pope Gelasius at the end of the fifth century asserting the duality of authority: "Two there are, august emperor, two authorities by which this world is chiefly ruled, the sacred authority of the priesthood and the royal power. . . . [I]n the order of religion, in matters concerning the reception and right administration of the heavenly sacraments, you ought to submit yourself rather than rule."[19] Though the matter was hardly settled by Gelasius, as the later history of struggles for dominance between pope and emperor shows, even these struggles reaffirmed Gelasius's distinction between the two spheres, temporal and spiritual. What was, then, at least in retrospect, settled by reference to Gelasius's statement was the distinction between religious and temporal authority. The tensions between representatives of these two spheres in subsequent centuries were not about erasing this distinction but over whether one would dominate the other, and if so, which one would dominate and which would be dominated. In line with this, the canonical debates over the idea of just war set in motion by Gratian ended with an unambiguous reservation of the right of *bellum iustum* to princes, temporal rulers with no temporal superiors, and this is the conception of the right of resort to just war that Aquinas, in turn, puts into theological context. Sovereignty thus defined was thus both a political and a moral concept.

It is important to make clear that the understanding of *ius gentium* found in the thought of this period looks back to the Roman usage, referring to the laws and associated rights of particular peoples. It thus served to support the rights of individual political communities against interference by others. Later, in the modern period, this same term, *ius gentium*, came to be used very differently: to refer to the "law of nations," an idea of a body of understandings common across national boundaries. I return later in this book to this shift in meaning, its context, and its importance.

Later Developments

The two concerns identified above, on the one hand for the moral behavior of individual Christians and on the other hand for the exercise of just rule, remained central to the development of normative Christian thinking about the use of force right through the Middle Ages and into the modern era, up through the Reformation and beyond. Catholic thinkers like Cajetan, Vitoria, and Suarez, and Protestant thinkers including Luther, Zwingli, Calvin, and others, like the canonists and theologians before them, mainly addressed the question of the just use of force in the context of thinking about the rights and responsibilities of government, Luther focusing more heavily on governmental authority, the Reformed theologians with more balance between such authority and the moral responsibilities of Christians living under it. In later Reformed thinkers like the Puritan theologian William Ames, the balance shifted more toward the rights and responsibilities of individual Christians not only regarding the use of force but toward government in general, and this has also been the line of development generally followed by the main line of Western thought, secular as well as religious, throughout the modern era. This can be seen in different ways, for example, in Hugo Grotius and in international law, where governing authority is understood in a de facto way, as morally neutral in character, and the focus is on the limits of use of force by the state; it can also be seen in the development of democratic theory from Locke onward, where the rights of government are tied explicitly to those of citizens and the use of force has to be described first of all in terms of the protection of those rights. These modern developments define the frame from within which we today instinctively approach matters of the use of force, the frame defined by the tradition associated with Grotius on the one hand and with Locke on the other. But in order to remain true to the idea of just war and its assumptions regarding good government and the individual moral life, we must look beyond this modern frame to the world of the passages quoted above, what they were taken to mean when they were first placed together, and how their meaning was amplified by other ideas.

In the context of that earlier world, it is important to stress the meaning and importance of the central ideas identified in the quoted passages and understood as requirements for the just use of force: sovereign authority, just cause, and right intention defined both negatively (via Augustine's listing of evil intentions) and positively (as the aim of establishing peace). These are fundamental deontological requirements, requirements that simultaneously limit the use of force to sovereign authority and impose binding duties on that authority: to ensure that the cause is one of the just causes identified, that the mindset is not one of evil intention, and that the purpose is to establish peace. It is essential, in the original definition of these requirements, that sovereign authority comes first, for then the remaining requirements impose obligations on the person or persons in such authority, including the obligation of determining whether those requirements are satisfied—whether the cause is just, whether the impetus for using force is rooted in evil intentions or in the purpose of serving the common good, whether the end at which the use of force aims is that of establishing peace or not. This understanding of the moral priorities disappears in just war thinking beginning early in the modern period, as sovereignty ceases being a moral concept and becomes simply a de facto characteristic of commonly recognized states. There were important reasons for this shift, but important losses also resulted from it. This shift continues to be manifest in lists of just war criteria in much recent just war thinking, religious and secular. Yet a moral component to sovereign authority—the idea that there are genuinely good and bad exercises of such authority—is an essential part of the whole theory of justified resort to force expressed in just war tradition, and a way needs to be found to think meaningfully about this again.

The ideas discussed above all belong to what later came to be called the *jus ad bellum*, the rules for resort to war. This is the part of just war tradition that has to do directly with the question of the nature of the idea of sovereignty. It is also the part of just war tradition that was influenced most directly by the Augustinian heritage. The conditions for justified resort to force—who might rightly employ force, for what causes, and with what intentions—were, in fact, the main concern of the twelfth- and thirteenth-century thinkers who shaped the scattered thoughts from the Augustinian heritage into a unified, consistent, systematic whole. Yet by the time this part of the tradition came together, there was also a nascent *jus in bello*, rules for conduct during war, centered on limits on certain weapons (weapons associated with mercenaries and with a tendency to cause indiscriminate and disproportionate harm) and a definition of noncombatant immunity defined by listings of persons who normally did not take part in war and who thus should not be harmed. This side of the developing idea of just war was influenced heavily by the chivalric tradition (indeed, the Latin term *jus in bello* is a translation of the chivalric term *loi d'armes*). During the twelfth and thirteenth centuries, these two aspects of just war tradition developed separately, being brought together in a larger synthesis by such writers as Henri Bonet and Christine de Pisan in the era of the Hundred Years War. This was the concept of just war known by such early modern theorists as the Spanish Catholic theologians Francisco de Vitoria and Francisco Suarez and by Protestants such as Luther, Zwingli, Calvin, and Ames, all of whom are discussed below.

The religious warfare of the sixteenth and early seventeenth centuries, though, imposed stresses on this inherited concept of just war from two directions. This had a devastating impact on the idea of sovereignty. First, in the sixteenth century, both Catholic and Protestant partisans put forward arguments for holy war.[20] They used the language and structures of just war tradition but fundamentally changed their meaning and priorities. In these holy war apologetics the focal question was whether a particular use of force served right religion (the one preferred by the particular apologist) or not. Just cause and right intention (understood as serving the cause of right religion against the enemy, represented as infidels, forces of the antichrist, or followers of Satan) thus became the most important categories for the holy war advocates, with the requirement of sovereign authority either subordinated to these or entirely subsumed within them. For one's legal sovereign might be of the other religion and an enemy to one's own. The core meaning of sovereign authority that traced back to Augustine, and which had been strongly fleshed out in the medieval canonistic debates about who in society has the right to authorize resort to force and who does not, was thus centrally challenged and undermined. On the holy war conception, the authority for resort to force was redefined as belonging to whoever would serve the cause of true religion by doing so. This played out in different ways in different parts of Europe—in the German lands of the Holy Roman Empire, in France, and in England—but with the same arguments being made in each. At the same time some, if not all, holy war advocates argued that warfare against the enemies of right religion should be entirely unrestrained, and whatever the theorists said, in practice these wars, understood as motivated, justified, and authorized by right religion, were often unrestrainedly bloody and cruel.

The other direction from which stress was imposed on the inherited traditions having to do with sovereignty and just war is exemplified by Grotius's *De iure belli ac pacis*. Written in the last years of the Thirty Years' War, which had begun as a religious war and attained the dubious distinction of being the bloodiest of a very bloody lot, this work described a regime of international relations in which sectarian religion had no place. Anticipating the conception of states and state sovereignty adopted in the Peace of Westphalia, Grotius described sovereignty in terms of de facto rule over a particular territory and its inhabitants and the international order in terms of ordered relationships among such territorially defined states. The right to engage in war, on the conception put forward by Grotius here, pertained to the obligation to defend the state's territory and the rights of its inhabitants against aggressors from outside. This conception was thus an early statement of the general nature and underlying assumptions of the state system as it took shape after the Peace of Westphalia and has since dominated. In it the idea of sovereignty defined in terms of the moral responsibility of the ruler to ensure the common good effectively disappeared, as sovereignty became a possession of the territorially defined state. The right of resort to force becomes recast, accordingly, as the right to defend that state. On this conception religion, or, more broadly, appeals to a higher conception of morality, should have no role in determining the justice of resort to force. At the same time, Grotius emphasized the rules for conduct in war. Parties to war were to observe the limits regardless of their opinion of the relative justice of their own cause or the relative injustice of the enemy's. Thus Grotius also anticipated the development of the law of war (today formally called the law of armed conflict) in customary and positive international law as a body of rules applicable to all parties in a conflict equally, regardless of the claimed justice or injustice on either side.

The medieval and early modern conception of sovereignty in terms of the moral obligation of those in political authority to serve the common good thus did not withstand the impact of these two opposing stresses: from the era of the wars of religion which cast the rights of rulers and ruled alike in terms of whether they professed the right religion, and from the reaction embodied in the work of Grotius and institutionalized in the

Peace of Westphalia, which, in order to reject and prevent warfare for religion, reduced sovereignty to de facto authority over a particular territory and the people who happened to inhabit it. The advocates of holy war sacrificed concern for the common good as a concept having to do with life in this world, replacing it with the idea that human worth depends entirely on religious profession. The Grotian-Westphalian conception also sacrificed the idea of sovereignty as service of the common good, focusing on the right of states to protect their territories and defining political authority in terms of the obligation to protect such territory. In the context of the seventeenth century, one might argue that concern for the welfare of the citizenry was included in this concept: Grotius, who developed his political thought in the context of argument for the rights of the Dutch people against Spanish overlordship, clearly made this assumption. But the power of this assumption waned even as dynastic ambitions grew, and the new understanding of sovereignty made no special claims on those in political authority to care for the rights and welfare of the people in the territory they governed. One result was the emergence of the absolutist state; another was to open the way for the exercise of political authority to become what in traditional terms was called tyranny. How to deal with this is centrally the problem of the meaning of sovereignty.

Notes

1. See my discussion of Augustine in Johnson, *The Quest for Peace*, 56–66.
2. Augustine, *Letter cxxxviii to Marcellus*. Cited from Thomas Aquinas, *Summa theologiae* II/II, Q. 40, A. 1; Gregory Reichberg, Henrik Syse, and Endre Begby, *The Ethics of War*, 177.
3. Augustine, *Contra Faustum*, xxii.75; ibid.
4. Augustine, *Questiones in Heptateuchum*, q. x, *Super Josue*; ibid.
5. Isidore, in Gratian, *Decretum*, part II, causa 23, question II, canon I; Reichberg, Syse, and Begby, *The Ethics of War*, 113.
6. Augustine, *Contra Faustum*, xxii.74; Reichberg, Syse, and Begby, *The Ethics of War*, 73.
7. Augustine, *Letter clxxxix to Boniface*; Aquinas, *Summa theologiae* II/II, Q. 40, A. 1, Reply Objection 3.
8. Romans 13:3–4 (RSV).
9. R. A. Markus, "Saint Augustine's Views," 1–13, at 7.
10. Ibid., 7–10.
11. Augustine, *City of God*, II.xxi.

12. Ibid., XIX.xiii.
13. See, for example, ibid., V.xv, xvii.
14. Markus, "Saint Augustine's Views," 10.
15. Weigel, *Tranquillitas Ordinis*, 28–29.
16. Tierney, "Religious Rights," 17–45, at 28.
17. Isidore, in Gratian, *Decretum*, part II, *causa* 23, question II, canon 1; Reichberg, Syse, and Begby, *The Ethics of War*, 113.
18. For fuller discussion of these conceptions of noncombatant immunity and their relationship, see Johnson, *Just War Tradition and the Restraint of War*, 131–50.
19. Quoted in Tierney, "Religious Rights," 22.
20. These arguments are not examined in this book, but see Johnson, *Ideology, Reason, and the Limitation of War*, chap. 2.

2

Sovereign Authority and the Justified Use of Force in Thomas Aquinas and His Early Modern Successors

The Thinking of Aquinas

Thomas Aquinas's concise treatment of the idea of just war is far better known today than the work of his intellectual predecessors, the twelfth- and thirteenth-century canonists on whom his conception depended. On the specific subject of sovereignty, the core of Aquinas's conception of the authority necessary for a just war, the canonists' debate had established the essential point that such authority belonged only to a temporal ruler with no temporal superior, for only such a person has no one else to whom to appeal for decisions as to justice in cases of conflict. Rather, such a ruler is in the position of being the final judge in such cases, and the ruler's judgment may include the decision that use of armed force is necessary to the establishment of justice. Aquinas begins where the canonists leave off, but he never moves far from the essential position they had defined.

Aquinas's Treatment of Just War: Justified Use of Force as an Instrument of Sovereignty

Aquinas's language in his discussion of just war has become widely familiar.[1] "In order for a war to be just," he writes, "three things are necessary." He then identifies these three conditions: the authority of a sovereign ruler (*auctoritas principis*, "princely authority"), just cause, and right intention. In the logic of his discussion the priority given here to the requirement of sovereign authority is not accidental but purposive: Only a sovereign ruler—a temporal ruler with no temporal superior, an understanding Aquinas took over from the conclusion of the canonical debates of the century before him—could undertake *bellum iustum*, "just war"; neither governing authorities with superiors over them nor private persons had the right to such use of force. But it was not the simple fact of sovereignty, on this account, that gave the prince with no superior the right to employ armed force; rather, the resort to arms had to be for a just cause, narrowly defined, and it had to serve the end of peace. The right of resort to arms given to the sovereign ruler came with the responsibility to use such force for justice and peace. Aquinas's account of just war, then, provides an important window into his understanding of the meaning of sovereignty: Sovereignty is government of a political community by a person or persons with final responsibility for the well-ordered justice and peace of that community, which Aquinas often rendered as its *bonum commune*, or "common good." In this frame the right of resort to arms is understood as a necessary tool that may need to be employed in the exercise of this responsibility.

The three requisites for a just war named by Aquinas are generally counted as four in present-day listings of the just war categories, because right intention as he describes it has two components, one positive and one negative. The positive side of right intention is the aim of peace, and present-day just war commentators generally list this as a distinct category within the *jus ad bellum*. The negative side is the avoidance of wrong intention. Aquinas puts it this way, using language borrowed from canon law: "True religion looks upon as peaceful those wars that are waged not for motives of aggrandizement, or cruelty, but with the object of securing peace, of punishing evildoers, and of uplifting the good." As he continues he treats the positive and negative components of right intention further, using language from Augustine to explain both wrong intentions (the passage from *Contra Faustum* xxii.74 quoted in chapter 1) and the end of peace (*Letter clxxxix to Boniface*, also quoted in chapter 1).

But let us think for a moment further about the passage borrowed from canon law, which describes right intention in this way: "the object of securing peace, of punishing evildoers, and of uplifting the good." Compare this with Aquinas's description of just cause, also using the language of Augustine: "A just war is wont to be described as one that avenges wrongs, when a nation or state has to be punished, for refusing to make amends for the wrongs inflicted by its subjects, or to restore what it has seized unjustly."[2] Now, canon law from Gratian onward included this statement, which renders just cause in terms of punishment of evil and recovery of that which has been wrongly taken, but as we have seen in chapter 1, it also included another statement on just cause from Isidore of Seville: "That war is just which is waged by an edict in order to regain what has been stolen or to repel the attack of enemies."[3] Aquinas surely knew this passage from Isidore; every canonist and theologian of his time would have. The standard medieval canonical listing of just causes, both before and after Aquinas, followed Gratian in combining Isidore and Augustine: defense against attack, punishment of evil, recovery of that which has been wrongly taken. Aquinas's usage is more, I think, than the expression of a preference for Augustine over Isidore, and he certainly justified action in self-defense elsewhere (notably in *Summa theologiae* II/II, Q. 64, A. 7). But the language he chooses for himself and borrows from others in his definition of both just cause and right intention in his discussion of just war is, I think, quite intentionally focused on the prevention of evil, the setting right of wrongs already committed, the punishment of evildoers, and overall the promotion of good. These are all precisely what a good ruler is to provide; they are not functions that allow anyone else in the political community to have recourse to force. By contrast, according to natural law, defense against attack is allowed for everyone. This was also explicitly recognized in canon law by the time Aquinas wrote. Any member of the political community may take up arms if necessary to defend against such attack, protecting himself and those in his own sphere of responsibility in this way. That the sovereign may also use force to defend the community as a whole follows from its being in his charge as well as from this general allowance of self-defense against attack. But the restoration of justice after an attack is another matter: This is the sovereign's responsibility, and is not shared by private individuals. This is what *bellum iustum*, "just war," is about: the vindication of justice in the service of good order and peace for the community.

So Aquinas, in discussing just war, singles out those specific justifying causes that set off the responsibility and the obligations of the person or persons in sovereign authority from those of any other person in the community. The result is a conception of just cause that is strikingly different from the one widely recognized as preeminent in present-day just war reasoning: self-defense. The emphasis on self-defense as the most obviously just cause for resort to war follows from international law, where it is effectively the only justifying cause available to individual states. Long before it was written into the United Nations Charter (Article 51), it was part of the reasoning of Grotius and was put in place by the state system created as a result of the Peace of Westphalia. But self-defense is not included in Aquinas's listing of just causes in "On War." He understood self-defense to be a natural right of any and all individuals and their communities, not a special justification needed for the community's use of force. So it is very important that Aquinas's listing of the requirements of just war begins with the requirement of sovereign authority; and so readers do not miss the significance of this requirement, its first priority among the necessities for a just war, he reminds us of this through the way he casts the requirements of just cause and right intention.

Here is how Aquinas defines the requirement of right authority in his definition of just war:

> For it is not the business of a private individual to declare war [*bellum*], because he can pursue his right (*ius suum prosequi*) before the judgment of his superior. Moreover, it is not the business of a private person to summon together the people, which has to be done in wartime. And as the care of the common weal is committed to those who are in authority, it is their business to watch over the common weal of the city, kingdom or province subject to them. And just as it is licit for them to have recourse to the material sword in defending that common weal against internal disturbances, as when they punish malefactors, according to the words of the Apostle (Romans 13:4): "He beareth not the sword in vain: for he is God's minister, an avenger to execute wrath upon him that doth evil"; so too, it is their business to have recourse to the sword of war in protecting the common weal against external enemies.[4]

Two things stand out here: the sharp distinction between the rights of the sovereign and those of private persons relating to the use of armed force, and the strong connection between the sovereign's right to use such force and his positive responsibilities as the one given charge for the commonweal. The former follows from the latter. In this Aquinas is absolutely at one with Augustine and the main line of Augustinian tradition in the Middle Ages. On this understanding there is a fundamental moral difference between the use of the sword by one in sovereign authority or on his behalf and the use of the sword by a private individual. The former may wage war, *bellum*, which is the use of the sword in the service of the common good; the latter may not. The private use of the sword, for medieval writers on just war, was *duellum*, literally a "duel," not war. Thus private persons could not wage just war, whatever the justice of their cause.

The reason, as given in the Augustinian tradition underlying medieval just war thinking, was that by definition such private use of the sword is tainted by private intentions, by *cupiditas*, or "self-love." Thus the fundamental requisite of a just war is that it be undertaken by sovereign authority, where its justice lies in its intention of serving the common good.

Aquinas's treatment of defense as just cause fits hand in glove with his interest in distinguishing between the use of the sword by sovereign authority and by a private person. He does not argue from the right of self-defense to the sovereign's right to the sword but rather cites the sovereign's responsibility to protect the commonweal. A private person may justly defend himself or others for whom he has responsibility when attacked; that is, in fact, the only justified use of the sword by private individuals that Aquinas appears ready to allow. But, as I suggest above, it is significant that when discussing war Aquinas does not speak of "defense against attack" but of "protecting the commonweal." What the sovereign is to defend against is both "internal disturbances" and "external enemies." His reasoning does not generalize from the right of self-defense against harm but particularizes from the sovereign's responsibility to seek the good of the society he governs. This is a very different sort of right to the sword from that allowed to private persons. Nor should one extend to the private individual other uses allowed only to the sovereign: to punish evil and to restore that which has been wrongly taken, whether the evildoers in either sort of case are internal to the society or external to it. Private individuals have no right of recourse to the sword for such reasons; they should instead appeal to their superior for justice, and it is the superior's "business," as Aquinas puts it, to seek to give it to them.

Rulers may, of course, in practice use the powers of their rule for their own private good, not for the commonweal of the community they govern. Doing this is tyranny, not the proper exercise of sovereign authority, and the power of such rulers over those governed does not equate to genuine authority over them. To observe this is to realize a further implication of the distinction between private and public authority, between persons not charged with the rights and responsibilities of sovereignty and those who are, and of the moral definition of sovereignty thus generated. With the two questions after "On War" in the *Summa theologiae*, Aquinas comes to this point in his discussion of sedition. He writes, "A tyrannical government is not just, because it is directed, not to the common good, but to the private good of the ruler. . . . Indeed it is the tyrant rather that is guilty of sedition, since he encourages discord and sedition among his subjects, that he may lord over them more securely; for this is tyranny, being conducive to the private good of the ruler, and to the injury of the multitude."[5]

It is no great distance from this to the argument of Calvin in the *Institutes of the Christian Religion* that inferior magistrates have the right to depose a tyrannical ruler, though Aquinas himself did not take this step.[6] For Aquinas (and for medieval and early modern just war thought as a whole), the sovereign's obligation to punish evildoing, which is not limited in his discussion to internal disturbances within his own political community but extends to externals as well, might justify the use of the sword against tyrannical rulers over other political communities. It is clear within this frame of thought that tyrants have no right to rule; they are in effect private persons and enemies of the common good, and they may be punished as evildoers because of their oppression of those under their power. This ability to name tyranny for what it is and the justification provided for removing and punishing tyrants are features of the medieval and early modern moral conception of sovereignty. It stands in stark contrast to the position of the post-Westphalian redefinition of sovereignty, which intentionally has to do with protecting the territorial integrity of a state, not with the nature of the rule meted out within it. Aquinas also devoted significant attention to the problem of tyranny in other writings and particularly in his *On Princely Government*, and I return to his treatment of this problem in this chapter.

In his discussion of just war, Aquinas's understanding is that it is the responsibility of the sovereign to uphold the good and seek to ensure the commonweal that gives him the right to employ the sword. The right to use armed force to punish evildoers and correct wrongs is the other side of the responsibility, in natural law and under God, to govern so as to serve the good. What Aquinas says on sovereign authority in the question "On War" points naturally to his short treatise *On Princely Government* (*De regimine principum*), where the prince's responsibilities are laid out in more detail.[7] This comparatively neglected work in Aquinas's corpus properly belongs to that stream in medieval political literature that culminates in Erasmus's *The Education of a Christian Prince*, which focuses on defining the exercise of ruling authority in fundamentally moral terms, terms determined by the good of the political community and the ruler's responsibility for seeking that good.[8] In the century after Aquinas the ruler's responsibility was described in the language of the Augustinian trilogy of order, justice, and peace by such otherwise different political writers as Marsilius of Padua (in *Defensor pacis*)[9] and Dante Alighieri (in *De monarchia*).[10] For both of these fourteenth-century writers, it is the ruler's responsibility to impose an order that embodies justice and thus produces and preserves peace, and the right to use armed force follows from this responsibility. The lines of thought found in these later writers and in Aquinas's discussion of princely rule and the sovereign's authority to use the sword all follow the Augustinian frame and lead toward the same end. Order alone is not enough, but it is a necessary prerequisite for justice and peace, and this justifies the use of armed force.

A respected European commentator on medieval Scholastic thought from early in the twentieth century, Alfred Vanderpol, remarked of the just war theory of Aquinas and of scholastic theology in general that it was focused on the punishment of evil as a way of serving *la justice vindicatif*, literally "vindicative"—not vindictive but vindicative—justice, the justice of vindication, of setting things right.[11] While this correlates closely with the two just causes for war named by Aquinas—the punishment of evil and restoring what has been wrongly taken—there is more to be said; Aquinas's conception of sovereign authority's justification for resort to armed force is put not only in such terms but also, more broadly and more positively, as "protecting the commonweal." In the present day, antipathies toward nuclear weapons and to various particular wars have led to distrust of the state and its power in various contexts, including in some recent writing on the idea of just war. The large state—and for some writers the United States in particular—has become the target of much suspicion. As part of this suspicion, the idea of the state and its power as a source of good has been forgotten or rejected, trumped by the idea that the state, in the pursuit of its self-interest, tends to use its power for injustice, not justice, for evil, not good. In such thinking the large state is inherently tyrannical. Hence its right to resort to armed force is regarded as something that needs to be curbed or rejected outright. But Aquinas, and other contributors to the conception of sovereignty I have been discussing, while recognizing the possibility of tyranny, defined the proper exercise of sovereignty as promoting good both within each individual society and in the relationships among such societies. Their fear was of private *cupiditas*, the wrong use of force that this might motivate, and the chaos and injustice that would result. In the absence of sovereign authority there is no proper political order, and this gives individuals freedom to pursue their private ends to the detriment of others.

One example of this view and its application, which antedates the coalescence of just war thinking that begins with Gratian and is manifest in Aquinas, is provided by the phenomenon known as the Peace of God, a movement that developed and flourished in southern and southwestern France during the late tenth and early eleventh centuries. These were regions in which a settled, peaceful life was routinely disrupted by violence from three kinds of sources: armed conflicts among local knights and barons over power and land, bullying and extortion by landless knights and men-at-arms employed by local lords, and robber bands living on the fringes of settled society who would periodically raid towns, villages, individual holdings, and travelers on the roads to take whatever they could for their own use. In short, these regions were the "wild west" of medieval France. The Peace of God movement was an attempt to deal with this chaotic, unjust state of affairs. It originated in the actions of regional councils of bishops, like the Council of Le Puy in 975 and that of Charroux in 989.[12] The action the bishops took aimed first at protecting the church's own—church buildings and their attached lands, clergy, religious, pilgrims on the road and their property. Soon the effort extended also to the protection of innocent townspeople, peasants on the land, travelers other than pilgrims, and the property of all these groups. The bishops' weapon was excommunication and the threat of damnation. This essentially religious movement quickly took on a temporal component, as the regional counts (a term that in this period designated a royally appointed official with regional authority and the armed forces to enforce that authority) took up the cause so as to extend royal authority and order into the affected regions by putting down violence and punishing those who were its source. The movement—whose name derives from the practice of the bishops' councils to adopt a statement establishing a "peace of God" around all the persons and properties identified for protection and levying anathemas against violators of this "peace"—struck a deep chord in medieval thought about politics and just war. Later in the just war tradition, this movement was the immediate, practical source of the idea of noncombatant immunity as defined in canon law (the categories of protected persons it named are effectively the same as those protected in the law of armed conflicts today), and it was also an important contributor to the canonical debate over the authority to wage war that we witness in Gratian and the two generations of canonists who built on his work, whose outcome Aquinas assumed and adopted in his question "On War."

For medieval thinkers on politics and the use of armed force, to put the matter succinctly, the immediate fear was chaos, which manifested itself in injustice and strife, and the answer these thinkers gave was to stress the responsibility of those in sovereign authority to establish the goods of political order, justice, and peace. Their fear was not of violence as such, as present-day critics of war would typically have it, but of violence in the service of private, selfish ends: all the things Augustine listed as "wrong intentions," that is, "the desire for harming, the cruelty of avenging, an unruly and implacable animosity, the lust of domination, and the like," a list the canonists and Aquinas prominently included in their own writings. Perhaps in an age when we have come to know the evil terrorism can do, we can understand this medieval perspective better than we could earlier. Yet the more general point to draw from the priority Aquinas, along with medieval just war tradition in general, gave to sovereign authority for the use of force is to look behind that requirement to its foundation in the conception of the good political community and the responsibility of the sovereign authority to support the commonweal and defend it against threats from both within and without. This is a lesson about how to think about politics and the meaning of sovereignty, one that is important not only for the medieval and early modern world, where this conception was formed and held sway, but also for our own society and its government as well as for other societies and the international realm as a whole in the present day.

Examining Aquinas's Understanding of Sovereignty More Closely

When Thomas Aquinas laid down "the authority of a prince" as the first requisite for a just use of armed force, he was reflecting the conclusion reached in the canonists' debates of the century and a quarter before him, that the authority for a just war is restricted to temporal rulers with no temporal superior. But the ranking he gave such authority also reflected the renewed attention given to the idea of natural law during that same period, according to which political community was conceived as a natural bonding among persons for their common good, with the ruler bearing the overall responsibility for maintaining and protecting that good. Broadly, this was a conception that in Christian thought traced back to Augustine, who described "the well-ordered concord of civic obedience and civic rule" both as the basis of peaceful life in the earthly city and as pointing toward the greater peace and concord to be experienced in the heavenly city (in *City of God* XIX.xvi–xvii), and whose counsel to the Roman governor of North Africa, Boniface, reminded him of his responsibility for the peace of those living in the area under his charge (in *Letter clxxxix*). But Aquinas's own thinking also benefited from Aristotle on nature and politics, with the latter's organic conception of the political community following the analogy of the family and the understanding of the ruler's role and responsibility in that context as like that of the father within the community of the family.

All this provides a background for understanding the role of the sovereign ruler in relation to the use of armed force, discussed in the previous section: Just war is for the good of the political community, for which the ruler has ultimate responsibility. This conception is also laid out in contexts within Aquinas's work where the focus is not the particular question of the use of armed force but the broader conception of life in a political community. Aquinas understood life in a political community as a result of the social character of humanity, which is rooted in human nature; his description of man as a "political and social animal" (*animal politicum et sociale*) expresses this basis for political life more completely than Aristotle's "political animal" (*politikon zoon*). The drive to live in communities is thus rooted in nature, and political community, building on this natural human drive, seeks the perfection of such a life. The well-being of any community's members depends on the well-being of the community as a whole. The degree to which any given political community succeeds in securing this well-being depends on its government, and this in turn places the focus on those who have ruling authority in the community. The entire conception of politics is thus ethical, and the responsibility of the ruler is defined in ethical terms as the responsibility for the common good of the whole political community governed. This general conception of sovereignty or rulership in terms of moral responsibility for the political community ruled thus provides the frame for understanding the priority given to "the authority of the prince" in Aquinas's listing of the requisites for a justified use of armed force and the overall description of just war, *bellum iustum*, in terms of the purpose of vindicating justice and securing peace. The good of the political community, the "commonweal," from which we derive the word "commonwealth," is thus summed up in terms of the creation and maintaining of a just and peaceful communal order, defending it against threats both internal and external. All this can be read from an analysis of the discussion of *bellum iustum*, but approaching the matter through the discussion of the ideal of good rule does more to uncover the general background and nature of the conception of sovereignty on which the discussion of just war rests.

Beyond what can be read about the conception of sovereignty as moral responsibility in Aquinas's question "On War" in the *Summa theologiae*, a fuller discussion of the role and responsibilities of the ruler is provided in his treatment of political life elsewhere in that work, in his brief didactic work *On Princely Government*, and in the examination of tyranny in his *Commentary on the Sentences of Peter Lombard*.

Of these, the last mentioned is the earliest, and what Aquinas says in it is useful for the conception of sovereignty mostly in that it introduces the matter of what constitutes rightful governing authority, though it does not fully elaborate its content. Here Aquinas first addresses the question of whether governing authority is of God or not, answering that there are two ways in which such authority is not of God: "either because of a defect in the person, because he is unworthy, or because of a defect in the means by which power was acquired." As to the last of these, he specifically goes on to deny that rightful authority exists where it has been seized by violence, unless subsequently the authority has been ratified "either by the consent of his subjects or by the authority of a superior." But in the first case, the ruler's authority is still to be obeyed despite the ruler's personal unworthiness, "because authority is always of God according to its form," so that "subjects are always bound to obey such rulers, however unworthy." Yet the duty of obedience disappears when "what is commanded by a ruler is contrary to the purpose for which the ruler was appointed," that is, when what is commanded is "contrary to the virtue which the ruler is ordained to foster and to preserve." In such a case a subject is not only not bound to obey but bound to disobey.[13]

But what is this "virtue" that constitutes the "purpose" of ruling authority? Aquinas does not explain this in his *Commentary on the Sentences*. But in his question "On Sedition" in the *Summa theologiae* (II/II, Q. 42) he returns to the matter of such virtue and the purpose of ruling authority in the context of tyranny, which consists in the misuse of such authority and the lack of virtue in the ruler. Here, as we have already seen in the previous section, Aquinas writes, "A tyrannical government is not just, because it is directed, not to the common good, but to the private good of the ruler. . . . Consequently there is no sedition in disturbing a government of this kind" unless the resistance causes greater harm to the common good than the tyrant's actions. Aquinas continues: "Indeed it is the tyrant rather that is guilty of sedition, since he encourages discord and sedition among his subjects, that he may lord over them more securely; for this is tyranny, being conducive to the private good of the ruler, and to the injury of the multitude."[14]

Aquinas comes at this matter from a somewhat different direction early in the *Summa theologiae*, where he is discussing political life in a broad frame: "The control of another who remains free, can take place when the former directs the latter to his own good, or to the common good."[15] A bit later he puts the matter more generally: "Government is the same thing as the direction of the governed to some end, that is, some good"; "so the first object of whoever rules a multitude is unity, or peace."[16] This in turn leads to his understanding of the value of political order: It is necessary for "regulating the conduct of man to his fellows with whom he has to live."[17] Law is the vehicle of such regulation, and its promulgation "is the business either of the whole community or of that political person whose duty is the care of the common good."[18] Later he clarifies his preference as to good government: "So the best ordering of power within a city or a kingdom is obtained when there is one virtuous head who commands over all; and who has under him others who govern virtuously; and when, furthermore, all participate in such government."[19] Still later, he characterizes the ruler as a judge, quoting Aristotle: "the judge is the embodiment of justice" and "the ruler is the custodian of justice."[20]

In all this Aquinas follows Aristotle closely, and his perspective is that of a philosophical and theological thinker defining in general terms what good government requires: a sovereign ruler who provides the members of the political community that is governed with order, justice, and peace, and thus serves the common good of that community. The conception of sovereign rule here is essentially moral in character, requiring virtue on the part of the ruler, with the character of that virtue defined by the ruler's discharge of his obligations to the community. Authority alone does not suffice; the end to which that authority acts is the critical factor. Tyranny is the opposite of proper sovereign rule, since the tyrant serves his own good, not that of the commonwealth he governs.

Good government, in Aquinas's thinking, follows from natural law. Though Aquinas recognized individual rights rooted in nature, his conception of the natural law, unlike the modern ideas that reshaped the conception of sovereignty beginning in the sixteenth century, came from reflection on "the Cosmos, from the notion of a world well ordered and graded of which law is the highest expression. . . . It expresses the dignity and power of man, who alone of created beings is called upon to participate intellectually and actively in the rational order of the universe."[21] Sovereign rule consists in this participation. The responsibility of the ruler to serve the common good arises out of the "dignity and power" to imitate the divine ordering of the universe in his or her own dealing with the political community governed and in its relationship with other political communities.

When Aquinas turned to putting this conception of the good ruler into the form of practical advice for good government, he did so at the request of the king of Cyprus and addressed the resulting work, *On Princely Government*, to him. Only the first book of the text as it now stands, and part of the second, clearly trace to Aquinas himself, but the first book is the part that deals with the issues we have been discussing, the issues central to the conception of sovereignty as responsibility for the common good, and thus the following discussion focuses here.

Much of Aquinas's attention in this book centers on his argument for the superiority of monarchy over the other two main kinds of government of political communities, aristocracy and democracy. This was by no means a singular concern for Aquinas but a discussion that had begun in the classical world and continued into the modern period, with different theorists analyzing the question somewhat differently and not always reaching the same conclusion. Aquinas's focus on monarchy in this volume also makes sense, given the specific character of the book as advice to its patron, a monarch. Aquinas's argument for monarchy, though, serves the broader end of laying out his understanding of good political rule as such and its definition in moral terms. He first argues for monarchy as that which "most nearly approaches a natural process,"[22] but he also argues for its superiority as "borne out by experience."[23] His reasoning reveals his major concern: that the government of the political community be characterized by unity. He admits certain positive features of government by aristocracy and even democratic polity as he understood them,[24] but his judgment is that government by one person (the linguistic meaning of monarchy being "rule by one") succeeds better than either of these in that it is inherently unitary. Unity considered alone, though, is not enough, for "tyranny, the corruption of monarchy, is the worst form of government."[25] The unity of government must be directed toward the common good of the community: "it is the duty of a king to provide for the good of the community."[26] The evil of tyranny is that, by contrast, "the personal aims of the ruler are sought to the detriment of the common welfare."[27] The best and most effective way to combat tyranny, Aquinas argues, is through monarchical rule, that is, unitary government that aims at the common good of the political community. Keeping this end and purpose of sovereign authority in mind also keeps the ruler from degenerating into a tyrant. Seeking to ensure that the ruler is a virtuous person is thus of major importance, whether (in cases in which the monarch is elected) by choosing the candidate least likely to become a tyrant or by positive instruction of the ruler in virtue (the purpose of books like *On Princely Government*). But moral rule is not only a matter of the ruler's character: Institutional structures within the political community are also important. In this same context Aquinas goes on, "Next, a monarchy should be so constituted that there is no opportunity for the king, once he is reigning, to become a tyrant. And, at the same time, the kingly power should be so restricted that he could not easily turn to tyranny."[28] That is, not only the character of the ruler but also the shaping of the institutions of the political community contribute to Aquinas's conception of sovereign rule in terms of the responsibility to ensure the common good of the community.

Nonetheless, tyranny may arise, and Aquinas observes that it is common. He discusses the matter of tyranny at various lengths in various contexts, and the overall scope of what he says well prepares the way for later treatment of this theme in the early modern period. His various discussions, though, pull in somewhat different ways. In *On Princely Government* he is rather cautious about how to respond to tyranny. Here he argues that the good of order in the political community is so fundamental that in cases of tyranny that is "not excessive," it is "wiser to tolerate it in limited measure, at least for a time, rather than to run the risk of even greater perils by opposing it."[29] In his *Commentary on the Sentences*, he had proceeded somewhat differently, making the matter of whether the people have the obligation to obey a tyrant hinge not on the degree of misrule but first of all on whether the tyrant has achieved his ruling authority rightfully or not. If the former, the people are bound to obey, "because authority is always from God as to its form, which is the cause of our duty to obey it."[30] If the latter, though, "anyone can reject such authority when the occasion arises."[31] If a tyrant who has come into his ruling authority wrongly commands something sinful, the subject's obligation is even stronger: "not only is one not bound to obey the ruler, but one is bound not to obey him."[32] In a third context, the discussion of sedition in the *Summa theologiae* (II/II, Q. 42) introduced in the previous section, Aquinas uses somewhat harsher language: sedition is always a mortal sin, and accordingly "a tyrannical government is not just, because it is directed, not to the common good, but to the private good of the ruler. . . . Consequently there is no sedition in disturbing a government of this kind [unless this produces more harm than the tyrant's rule]. Indeed it is the tyrant rather who is guilty of sedition, since he encourages discord and sedition among his subjects, that he may lord over them more securely; for this is tyranny, being conducive to the private good of the ruler, and to the injury of the multitude."[33] "There is no sedition in disturbing a government of this kind." This is a rather different conclusion from those reached in either the *Commentary on the Sentences* or *On Princely Government*. The furthest Aquinas goes in the latter context is his comment, "It seems . . . that the remedy against the evils of tyranny lies rather in the hands of public authority than in the private judgment of individuals."[34] This observation and his subsequent explanatory example sound not unlike the position familiarly associated with Calvin some three hundred years later, that "lesser magistrates" in a political community might rightly depose a tyrannical ruler. But in the *Commentary on the Sentences* and in *On Princely Government* he seems to be saying much less; and indeed, his final word on the matter in *On Princely Government* is that "when there is no hope of human aid against tyranny, recourse must be made to God."[35] Yet this particular conclusion leaves somewhat open the nature of the human aid that might be provided: should it be that of the lesser authorities within the political community, whose own authority rests on their responsibility for the good of the community, or should it be, in cases in which a tyrannical ruler has a superior, that the superior should remove the tyrant, or should it be, as seems a possible reading of the discussions of just war and sedition in the *Summa theologiae*, Questions 40 and 42, that the tyrant's violations of justice make him subject to just rulers of other political communities, who thereby have the right to remove him to defend against the threat to the good of their own communities, a position that seems to correspond to present-day international law in significant ways? Aquinas thus does not provide a clear answer, though his various discussions map the territory of later discussions rather completely.

For the purpose of our examination of the conception of sovereignty, in any case, the question of tyrannical rule and how to deal with it serves in the first place to establish the idea of sovereignty as moral responsibility for the common good, in opposition to tyranny as the exploitation of ruling authority and power for personal gain. This latter definition would encompass various forms of government that are today challenged as violating the fundamental human rights of some or all those governed. Aquinas may have lived seven and a half centuries ago, but the defective forms of political life he describes sound remarkably like those of today.

Three Early Modern Interpreters of Aquinas on War: Cajetan, Vitoria, and Suarez

The conception of just war laid out by Thomas Aquinas in the *Summa theologiae* not only well summarized the position reached in canonical thought over the century and a quarter before he wrote, but also became the standard conception of just war and lasted well into and through the period of religious warfare that followed on the Protestant Reformation. By the time Aquinas wrote his question "On War," the canonists had said all they would say on the matter. After Aquinas, other medieval theologians wrote on the subject—sometimes differing from him—but his was the conception that remained the norm. The main new development in medieval just war thinking after Aquinas came from a different source, the writers who during the era of the Hundred Years' War (the late fourteenth century and early fifteenth) joined the chivalric "law of arms" (rendered in Latin as *jus in bello*) to Aquinas's summary of the requirements for a decision as to a just war (later termed the *jus ad bellum*), principally Honoré Bonet and Christine de Pisan. This combined conception was then passed on into the debates over warfare in the early modern period.

During the late Middle Ages Aquinas's particular formulation of just war, including his conception of the role of the sovereign in relation to the justness of the use of armed force, was accepted but not much examined as to its content. Beginning in the early sixteenth century, though, this began to change, as a succession of theologians undertook explicitly to recover Aquinas's thinking in detail and to interpret it in light of the changed historical conditions, intellectual, political, and military. The first of these "Neo-Scholastics" was Thomas de Vio (1468–1534), known as Cajetan, after his birthplace, the Italian city of Gaeta. Cajetan, like Aquinas, was a Dominican. Then came three Spanish theologians, also Dominicans, associated with the University of Salamanca: Francisco de Vitoria (1492–1546), Domingo de Soto (1494–1560), and Luis de Molina (1535–1600). Of these, Vitoria made the most important and lasting contribution. The last major figure in this movement was the Spanish Jesuit Francisco Suarez (1548–1617), who, though connected intellectually to the thinking of Cajetan and Vitoria, lived in very different times, the era of the post-Reformation wars of religion. Suarez, whose lifetime overlapped with those of Gentili, Althusius, Ames, and Grotius, all of whom engaged in reflection on the idea of just war, was the last major Catholic theologian to develop a theoretical account of just war until Catholic thinkers again began to pay attention to the topic in the latter part of the twentieth century. But that is a story for another context; here our focus is on the way these later thinkers in the Scholastic tradition used and modified the thinking of Thomas Aquinas on sovereignty and the use of armed force. In the discussion that follows, I focus on Cajetan, Vitoria, and Suarez.

Cajetan

Cajetan was highly influential in the development of Scholastic thinking, and particularly the idea of just war, in the sixteenth century and seventeenth. This owed mainly to his commentary on Aquinas's *Summa theologiae*, which was completed in 1517. His discussion of Aquinas's question "On War" introduced the concept of perfect versus imperfect political communities, which was then employed by Vitoria and other later writers, including the English Puritan theologian William Ames, who is treated in the following chapter.

In understanding the meaning of a text, the context matters enormously. In the first article of the question "On War," Aquinas names "the authority of a prince" as the first requirement for a just war. In his own time the meaning of this was plain, for the debates among the canonists of the latter part of the twelfth century and the first part of the thirteenth over the nature of the necessary authority had identified it as possessed only by temporal princes having no temporal superior. Aquinas's summary of the conditions needed for a just war directly reflects and summarizes the conclusions reached by the canonists during these debates. Cajetan's discussion of Aquinas's text, though, seems to reflect a different context, one in which the question of the necessary authority is not fully resolved, and so he undertakes to settle it. This leads him to make three distinctions: between defensive and offensive war, between perfect and imperfect political communities, and between the use of force internally within such communities against criminal behavior and externally against other such communities. The second of these is the most fundamental, and it is most useful to begin with it.

First a word about terminology. Cajetan, writing in Latin, used the word *respublica*, which yields the modern word "republic," yet he definitely did not intend a republic in the modern sense. His meaning is closer to the literal Latin: a "public entity," as opposed to a private one like a family. I prefer the term "political community" for this; the translation cited here (that of Reichberg, Syse, and Begby), though, employs the term "commonwealth" both for Cajetan and for later writers including Vitoria and Ames (both of whom also wrote in Latin). When citing these authors in the discussion below, I follow the usage in the translation provided; elsewhere, I also use the term "political community."

To clarify the ambiguity he finds in Aquinas's requirement of "the authority of a prince" for there to be a just war, Cajetan writes, "When therefore it is said that to declare a just war the authority of the prince is required, this should be understood either of a perfect commonwealth, or of someone perfectly standing for a commonwealth, . . . as for example kings or other similar rulers. . . . We say that there are two sorts of princes. Some are indeed heads and rulers unconditionally, perfectly standing for a commonwealth. Others are heads and rulers conditionally, imperfectly standing for a commonwealth."[36] In removing the ambiguity he finds in Aquinas's language, Cajetan unfortunately introduces an ambiguity of his own by applying the terms "perfect" and "imperfect" to both the ruler and the commonwealth. Vitoria clears up the matter by speaking of perfect and imperfect commonwealths only. In Cajetan, though, a close reading of his discussion shows that in the end the ambiguity in his usage does not amount to an ambiguity in substance: There are commonwealths whose rulers have no superior and other commonwealths whose rulers do have one or more superiors; his point is the same as that of Aquinas and the canonists before him, that only the former have the authority needed for a just war.

But this is not the whole story, since Cajetan also introduces the other two distinctions identified above. The first of these, that between defensive and offensive war, is also one that Aquinas did not explicitly address, because it had been settled in canon law not long before he wrote by a decretal from Pope Innocent IV in which he wrote the following: "It is permissible for anyone to wage war in self-defense or to protect property. Nor is this properly called 'war' (*bellum*) but rather 'defense' (*defensio*)." He continued by clarifying that defense must be "on the spot," that is, an immediate response. The right of defense does not extend to the right of later punishment or restitution; that is a matter for the prince, a matter for *bellum*.[37] Cajetan makes essentially the same points: "For a private person has . . . the right to 'repel force by force with the moderation of a blameless defense.' But it is beyond 'the moderation of blameless defense' for a private person to seek revenge for himself or others."[38] The right of defense also extends to the prince of an imperfect commonwealth; yet inside his own jurisdiction, such a prince also has the right "to exact revenge for injuries to itself or its members." That is, for Cajetan even the ruler of an imperfect political community, one that is a part of a larger perfect political community (such as a duke, marquis, or count within a kingdom, he suggests), has "vindicative authority" within his own jurisdiction, "but only insofar as it is delegated to them" by the head of the larger community.[39] Aquinas did not discuss such a possibility; for him, "vindicative authority" finally lies only with the temporal ruler who has no temporal superior. Cajetan's position likely reflects the historically grounded practice he knew. But there is another difference between Aquinas and Cajetan that appears in this connection: For Aquinas *bellum iustum*, the use of armed force by a temporal ruler with no temporal superior to recover that which has been wrongly taken or to punish evildoing (that is, in Cajetan's terminology, to vindicate justice) and with the intention of restoring a disordered peace, refers to the use of such force both internal to the ruler's own society and externally, against threats and disturbances from persons or political communities outside its borders. Cajetan distinguishes these in his discussion, though he continues to use the word *bellum*, "war," for both. Later writers would increasingly reserve the latter term for armed conflicts between political communities, and the use of force within such communities would be described in terms of policing.

Cajetan's casting of the issues in this way leads him to his third distinction, that between defensive and offensive war. Again, Aquinas finds no need to make such a distinction. But for Cajetan, it is necessary because the most that is allowed to rulers with superiors is to use armed force in defense against external attack and to vindicate justice within their own particular domains. Other uses of force are reserved for those rulers without any superior. Cajetan thus distinguishes between defensive and offensive warfare, with the rulers of imperfect commonwealths allowed only defensive warfare but only rulers of perfect commonwealths allowed both defensive and offensive warfare. What he means by offensive warfare turns out to be the vindication of justice against others over whom they have authority only because of some fault of those others, that is, because they have done some wrong that needs to be set right.[40]

The result of all this is at once to retrace and reaffirm steps already taken in earlier just war thinking, to deal with the realities of political communities, their governance, and their interrelations in his own time, and to put on the table certain conceptions that would form the frame for later discussions of rulership and the right to employ armed force. Sovereignty for Cajetan turns out to be the same as it was for Aquinas and the canonists whose work his own reflected: It consists in having final responsibility for the common good of the political community governed. (Common good = common weal, hence the term "commonwealth.") Sovereignty as treated by Cajetan is thus essentially moral in character, tied to this responsibility and the duty to discharge it. Though Vitoria and later writers adopted Cajetan's language of perfect and imperfect commonwealths, they also introduced an idea that is not found in Cajetan's thought but that his language opened the door to: the idea that the ruler acts as agent for the commonwealth, and that sovereignty is a quality of the commonwealth—the political community—itself, exercised only by the ruler on behalf of that community.

Vitoria

As in the case of Cajetan, the fundamental shape and content of Vitoria's thought on just war, and especially his treatment of sovereignty and the use of armed force, follow Aquinas's formulation; the differences for Vitoria are in certain inferences and extrapolations he draws that reflect his own historical and intellectual context. Like Aquinas, Vitoria begins his examination of the conditions required for a just war with the requirement of sovereign authority, and then goes on to what constitutes just cause. His discussion of the latter involves him in Aquinas's third condition, right intention, which he does not treat separately; rather, after examining the first two conditions, he turns to the question of right conduct in war. All this is in Question 1 of his *De jure belli*; in Question 2 he focuses in more detail on matters concerning justice in the resort to war, and in Question 3 he returns for a close look at the conduct allowed in a just war. In these two latter questions he goes well beyond what Aquinas discusses in his question "On War"; Vitoria's particular emphasis on the matter of right conduct reflects the synthesis achieved in the century before him between matters that had earlier been treated largely separately: resort to the use of armed force on behalf of the political community, which focused centrally on the role of the sovereign and his responsibility for the public good; and conduct in the use of force thus justified, which focused on the warrior himself, his intention, and his behavior while under arms. But I suggest that Vitoria's stress on the matter of conduct in just war also reflects the changes in the nature of armies already well advanced by his time: the growth of armies of common men, replacing the medieval norm of armies of men of the knightly class, and the growing destructiveness of war brought about by larger armies and the introduction of gunpowder and firearms. The changing nature of war also affected everyone else who wrote on the idea of just war in this period, right down through Grotius and those he influenced, and I treat it more fully in the next chapter.[41]

As for the detail of Vitoria's analysis and argument, on the question of authority for war Vitoria answers through three propositions: (1) "Any person, even a private citizen, may declare and wage defensive war." (2) "Second, any commonwealth has the authority to declare and wage war." (3) "Third, in this matter the prince has the same authority as the commonwealth."[42] On the matter of the distinction between private and public uses of armed force he follows the tradition closely:

> The difference between a private person and the commonwealth is that the private person has . . . the right to defend himself and his property, but does not have the right to avenge injury, nor even, indeed, to seize back property which has been taken from him in the past. Self-defence must be a response to immediate danger, made in the heat of the moment or *incontinenti* as the lawyers say. Once the immediate necessity of defence has passed, there is no longer any license for war. . . . The commonwealth, on the other hand, has the authority not only to defend itself, but also to avenge and punish injuries

> done to itself and its members. . . . The commonwealth cannot sufficiently guard the public good and its own stability unless it is able to avenge injuries and teach its enemies a lesson. . . . So it is necessary for the proper administration of human affairs that this authority should be granted to the commonwealth.[43]

Aquinas had put this in simpler and more compact language: Just cause for war (for him this meant the use of armed force on sovereign public authority beyond the right of defense) includes the rights of retaking what has been wrongly taken and the punishment of evildoing. Both follow directly from natural law. Vitoria, though, goes further and adds a prudential argument, shifting the focus from the maintenance of justice (Aquinas's focus) to the stability of the commonwealth itself, that is, its use of force to protect itself as a political community able to ensure the public good for its members. This bears directly on how Vitoria treats the role of the ruler. For Aquinas the touchstone is Romans 13:4: the prince is "minister of God, a revenger to execute wrath on him who does evil." Vitoria also quotes this passage and notes Aquinas's use of it, but Vitoria cites it in connection with his argument that Christians may engage in just war,[44] whereas Aquinas cites it in explaining the sovereign's authority to use armed force, a rather different context.

In the following section Vitoria fills out the implications of his shift in understanding the issues in two ways: first, by explicitly defining the role of the prince not as the primary actor, but as an agent of the commonwealth in the decision to use armed force; second, by clarifying what it is in the nature of the commonwealth that gives it the right to use such force. As to the first, he writes: "The prince must be chosen by the commonwealth, therefore he is the authorized representative of the commonwealth."[45] To be sure, the sentence that immediately follows insists, "where the commonwealth has a legitimate prince, all authority rests in his hands"; yet the source of that authority remains the commonwealth as a whole. This is very different from the conception found in Aquinas and the earlier just war tradition, that the prince receives authority to govern directly from God, and he acts as God's "minister." As to the second matter, what it is in the nature of the commonwealth that gives it the right to use armed force, Vitoria clarifies this by introducing his version of the concept of a "perfect community" (*perfecta communitas*), as opposed to an "imperfect" one: "A perfect community or commonwealth is . . . one which is complete in itself; that is, one that is not part of another commonwealth, but has its own laws, its own independent policy, and its own magistrates."[46] It follows, he goes on, that "princelings who are not sovereigns of independent commonwealths . . . cannot declare or wage war." But despite this effort at precision, Vitoria admits that the final arbiter is custom: "Despite all this, however, it must be admitted that for the most part these matters are done according to the law of nations or human law; and therefore, custom may establish the right and authority to wage war. If any city or prince has obtained the customary right to wage war on their own account, then this right may not be contested, even if in other respects the commonwealth is not independent."[47]

It is certainly worth taking a closer look at Vitoria's shift in reasoning and language and asking what has been gained and lost by it. The first thing to say is that the idea that the ruler's position depends on the larger community of those governed is not itself a new idea. When medieval writers on just war used the language of Romans 13:4, that the prince is "minister of God," they were not asserting anything like the later idea of the divine right of kings or a conception of exalted sovereignty like that described by Jean Bodin or embodied in Hobbes's Leviathan. Rather, they were thinking of the nature of princely rule within the context, on the one hand, of the recovered Roman legal doctrine of the sovereignty of the people and, on the other hand, of the customs in the Germanic tradition of rulership that provided for a good deal of flexibility in the establishing of supreme rule and the possibility that such rule could be taken away if abused or even mishandled. The former was an idea that reasserted itself in Spanish political thought in the sixteenth century. Bernice Hamilton observes that the political community as conceived then "was not created by a pact of men [as in later social contract thought], but was a natural association, exercising its inherent right to govern itself."[48] Commenting on the latter, Christopher Dawson speaks of "the direct personal bond of loyalty and mutual aid between the warrior and his chief, and that of service and protection between the serf and his lord."[49] He is referring specifically to the conditions of the eleventh century here but argues that the understanding of the relationships within feudal society came out of this. A bit later, when he turns to the rise of the medieval cities and gilds, Dawson describes a somewhat different conception: "This doctrine of society [developed in the cities and gilds] involves the principle of hierarchical subordination at every stage, but unlike the Aristotelian theory it does not involve total subordination or the institution of slavery. For every individual member of the whole is an end in himself, and his particular *officium* or *ministerium* is not merely a compulsory social task but a way of the service of God through which he shares in the common life of the whole body."[50] That is, each member of such communities is, in his own particular way, a "minister of God" and is answerable to him; that includes the person holding and wielding sovereign authority over the community. A similar point is made by Johann Huizinga in discussing the hierarchic conception of society in the Middle Ages, where he speaks of "the social importance of the common people" as the basis of the well-being of society as a whole.[51]

The importance of Vitoria's shift in language, locating sovereign authority in the political community rather than in its ruler, is not, then, in its implicit claim that the position of the ruler depends on the support of the community, for that idea was already present in medieval thinking; rather, the importance in the change is that Vitoria describes the ruler's authority not as a moral responsibility owed through nature to God but as a political responsibility owed to the community governed. The point of the sovereignty of the political community as to the right to use armed force is, moreover, for Vitoria located in the right of self-preservation, whereas medieval writers on just war thought of the use of force first of all in terms of the vindication of justice, a conception that still persists as late as Cajetan. Though Vitoria also uses this language frequently, the logic of his position puts new emphasis on self-defense and builds from this to the right to punish malefactors. We see this strikingly in a further extension Vitoria makes to the right to wage war, in a paragraph that immediately follows the last one quoted above: If, within a perfect commonwealth, one of its parts is attacked by another one, and the supreme ruler does not respond or does not do so adequately, then the part attacked has not only the right to use arms to defend itself, "but may also carry the war into its attacker's territory and teach its enemies a lesson. . . . Otherwise the injured party would have no adequate self-defence. . . . By the same argument, even a private individual may attack his enemy if there is no other way open to him of defending himself against harm."[52]

This is precisely the line of argument later made by Grotius. It locates sovereignty in the political community itself and defines the right to use armed force in terms of the right of self-defense of that community's borders, its people, and their "ancient laws and privileges," rather than locating this right in the moral obligation of the temporal ruler who bears ultimate responsibility for the common good of the community governed to respond to violations of justice and correct them, thereby protecting and maintaining the good order of the community and its peace.

This is a major change in the conception of sovereignty. Grotius's work, a century after Vitoria, makes this new understanding the basis of a theory of international order aimed at the protection of political communities and the individual and social rights and freedoms of their inhabitants against threats from rulers who would impose on them an order based on their own beliefs. That seems to be Vitoria's principal aim too. In the very next section, he asks, "What are the permissible reasons and causes of just war?" and begins by stating three limiting propositions: "First, difference of religion cannot be a cause of just war. . . . Second, enlargement of empire cannot be a cause of just war. . . . Third, the personal glory or convenience of the prince is not a cause of just war." Only then does he state the reason that was at the core of the traditional idea of just cause: "Fourth, the sole and only just cause for waging war is when harm has been inflicted."[53] A bit later, in Question 2, he imposes further restraints on any tendency the prince may have to act alone. In Article 1 he asks, "Whether it is enough for the just war that the prince should believe that his cause is just?" and answers in the negative: "First, this is not always enough. . . . Any man's opinion is not sufficient to make an action good; it must be an opinion formed according to the judgment of a wise man. . . . It would otherwise follow that most wars would be just on both sides. . . . Second, for the just war it is necessary to examine the justice and causes of war with great care, and listen to the arguments of the opponents." In Article 2 he amplifies this latter point: "All senators and territorial magnates, and in general all those who are admitted or called [to] or of their own accord attend the public or royal council are in duty bound to examine the cause of just war," and the ruler should listen to their counsel, because he "is not capable of examining the causes of war on his own."[54] The traditional conception of the prince's exercise of responsibility was, by contrast, to describe him as the supreme judge, focusing on his responsibility to make the decision on his own whether the resort to arms would serve justice. For Vitoria the final judgment may still rest with him, but he is bound on all sides by cautions of his own fallibility, his need to avoid purely personal judgments that might be self-serving, and the obligation to seek out and listen to the judgments of others. Finally, as noted above, he acts not on the basis of his own moral responsibility before nature and God, but as an agent of the community as a whole. Yet what their own responsibility is seems truncated to defense of themselves and of the community; necessity to act out of defense trumps other restrictions. Aiming at restricting the right to war, this opens a long-term Pandora's box.

Suarez

Suarez is the last major Catholic theologian to treat the subject of just war systematically and in depth until the latter part of the twentieth century. While his treatment reflects the conditions and thinking of his own era, it remains deeply anchored in the classic medieval understanding of just war shaped by the twelfth- and thirteenth-century canonists and Aquinas; and especially on the important subjects of the necessary authority for a just resort to armed force, just cause, and the aim of just war, he is closer to the position of the medieval tradition than to the thinking of Vitoria (who came before him) and of his contemporaries Gentili, Ames, and Grotius, all treated in the next chapter. Suarez's disputation "On War" (*De bello*) thus provides a strong reminder of the earlier tradition in a context in which elements of that tradition were being reexamined and reconceived by many, and, before many years had passed after his death, the whole conception of just war would be redefined.

He begins *De bello* with a strong, terse rejection of the idea that war is intrinsically evil, a passage contemporary Catholic thinkers enamored of the US Catholic bishops' preoccupation with the conception of war as prima facie morally wrong might well read and reflect upon. Then, following the order of the necessary conditions for just war as laid out by Aquinas, he turns to the question of the authority necessary for just war and then to the question of just cause. Like Vitoria, he treats Aquinas's third condition, right intention (defined by him in terms of the rejection of certain evil intentions and the affirmation of the final end of peace), in the context of his discussion of the first two, authority and just cause, but unlike Vitoria, he dwells on the matter of intention at some length, developing his argument against warfare for religion here, before turning to the matter of proper conduct in a just war, as Vitoria also does.

His statement on the authority necessary for a just war concisely focuses the position reached by the canonists and summarized in Aquinas's question "On War":

> I hold that a supreme prince (*supremus princeps*) who has no superior in temporal affairs, or a commonwealth that has retained for itself a like perfection, has by natural law (*iure naturale*) legitimate power to declare war. . . . The power of declaring such a war must rest with someone; and therefore it must rest, most of all, with the possessor of supreme power, for it is particularly his function to protect the commonwealth, and to command inferior authorities.
>
> A second reason is that the power of declaring war is (so to speak) a power of jurisdiction, the exercise of which pertains to vindicative justice, which is especially necessary to a commonwealth for the purpose of constraining others. Hence, just as the supreme prince may punish his own subjects when they harm others, so may he avenge himself on another prince or commonwealth, that, by reason of some offence, has become subject to him.[55]

The idea of the purpose of just war as vindicative justice, which Suarez spells out more fully in his discussion of just cause, draws attention to the importance of the judicial function of just war that first appears in this connection in the *Decretum*. The emphasis on defense found in Vitoria is not given voice here: Suarez describes the use of justified force in a well-ordered political community whose ruler understands well his role in maintaining justice and his responsibility to do so for the common good. Though he does not cite Romans 13:4 in this context, its terms loom over what he says: The prince is God's minister and can use the power of the sword to punish evildoers.

In the next paragraph Suarez clarifies what he has said about the power of a commonwealth to engage in just war, giving more clarity than had Vitoria on the matter of the relation of the commonwealth's authority to that of the supreme ruler:

> I used the words "or a commonwealth," in order that I might include every kind of regime. . . . Nevertheless, of a monarchical regime it must be noted that after a commonwealth has transferred its power to a single individual, it is not allowed to declare war against his will, since it no longer enjoys supremacy; unless perchance the prince should be so negligent in avenging or defending the commonwealth as to cause public and very grave harm to that commonwealth. In such a case the commonwealth as a whole may take vengeance on the prince, depriving him of his authority, for the

> commonwealth is always regarded as retaining this power within itself, if the prince fails in his duty.[56]

In this paragraph Suarez with his typical concision affirms the tradition's emphasis on the responsibility of the ruler himself regarding the use of armed force in the service of the common good, while asserting the right of the commonwealth as a whole to depose him if he fails in that responsibility.

He next turns to the rights of inferior princes and imperfect commonwealths regarding the use of armed force on their own agency: They may do so in defense, but they may not go beyond a proportionate use of force for this purpose. Taking up a possibility that, for Vitoria, extended the rights pertaining to the defensive use of force—namely, an attack on one part of a perfect commonwealth by another—Suarez rejects Vitoria's conclusion: "Nevertheless this course of action [allowed by Vitoria] is not [entirely] commendable, especially when the conflict occurs between two parts of the same commonwealth.... For to avenge oneself, on one's own private authority, is intrinsically evil, and tumults and wars might easily be stirred up within a commonwealth on this pretext."[57]

On another matter, what constitutes a complete or perfect commonwealth and the restriction of the right to resort to war to such political communities or their rulers, he takes a line reminiscent of Vitoria's, noting that sometimes the right of just resort to force is determined by customary usage: "All kings are in this respect supreme," Suarez writes, and "many counts also claim this supreme power." He goes on, "Consequently, the issue depends on the mode of jurisdiction exercised by each particular prince, or commonwealth," specifically, whether there exists in the realm "a tribunal before which all cases of litigation are decided" with no right of higher appeal. But sometimes, he continues, this state of affairs has come about "accidentally." Suarez does not, though, connect this state of affairs to the right to use armed force beyond what is allowed by defense (as Vitoria does), but rather refers it to the power that a "complete" commonwealth has over its own king, to resist and depose him "if he lapses into tyranny."[58]

When Suarez turns to the subject of just cause he begins with the classic requirement: that the "just and sufficient reason for war is the infliction of a grave injury that cannot be avenged or repaired in any other way." Only in explaining this does he introduce the idea of self-defense:

"that the commonwealth may protect itself from harm."[59] In further clarification of the main idea, he notes that there are three main kinds of injuries that can provide cause for a just war: One is "the seizure by a prince of another's property, and his refusal to restore it." This directly restates the classic idea, taken over by Augustine from Roman law and restated by Gratian and Aquinas from Augustine, of the recovery of that which has been wrongly taken. But the second category Suarez names goes to a different source, the idea of rights and their violation: "Another [type of injury] would be his denial, without reasonable cause, of the common rights of nations, such as the right of transit over highways, trading in common, etc." (Vitoria had used this same reasoning to argue that the Spanish have just cause for war against the Indians when the latter deny missionaries the right of free passage.)[60] But this reasoning also shows how the idea of the rights of nations, based on the conception of rights that had come into medieval European thought at the same time as the idea of just war and was tied to it intellectually and culturally, had by the early modern period produced a fundamental conception of the law of nations. In citing the violation of these rights as an injury sufficient to justify war, Suarez is quite a man of the modern age. But the language he uses for the third kind of injury justifying resort to war again reflects the Middle Ages: "a grave injury to one's reputation or honor."

All the above falls under Suarez's explanation of the idea that doing a grave injury can provide a cause for just war. But this is not all: "A war may also be justified on the ground that he who has inflicted an injury should be justly punished, if he refuses to give just satisfaction for that injury, without resort to war."[61] Again, this sorting out of what constitutes just cause follows the Augustinian model found in both Gratian and Aquinas, whereby there are two just causes, the second of which is the punishment of evildoing. How this justifies one supreme authority in making war on another Suarez also states in the language of the classic just war tradition: The power of punishment is not to be found in any superior to such authorities, "for we assume that these commonwealths have no commonly acknowledged superior; therefore, the power in question must reside in the supreme prince of the injured commonwealth, to whom, by reason of that injury, the opposing prince is made subject." War, then, is "in place of a tribunal administering just punishment."

Suarez, like Vitoria, went out of his way to deny that difference of religion and the desire to enforce true religion provide just cause for war. For

Vitoria the context was the Spanish conquest of the New World and the question of whether war could be made against the Indians for this reason. For Suarez, the context was more immediate, for his life spanned the period of the worst of the post-Reformation wars of religion. He forthrightly denies that such appeals to religion provide just cause for war, calling each form of this appeal a "false ground."[62] He concludes with a summary reference back to the traditional just war conception that every just cause for war must be rooted in natural law and justice thus defined. This was an idea first formed in the canonical debates of the early thirteenth century, when the context was that of the early Crusades; now, in the context of other wars in which each side attempted to punish the other because of a different religion and to impose "true" religion on the other, Suarez wastes little space rejecting the reasoning behind this and reaffirming where the canonists had come out during the earlier debates over religious cause for war.

Like Vitoria before him, Suarez gives significant attention to the matter of the supreme ruler's need to reach a high degree of certitude before engaging in war, a certitude founded on the counsel of others and not only on his own judgment. Where Vitoria had argued only that the prince should seek such counsel, Suarez says that he must do so: "Supreme princes are bound to submit the matter [of war] to the decision of good men." But at the same time, the final decision is his alone, for only he has the overall responsibility for the society's common good and the maintenance of justice relative to it.[63]

In the spirit of his age, Suarez also gives significant attention to the question of right conduct in war.[64] His discussion extends over not only what may be done *in bello* but also what may be done *post bellum*; in the thinking of the sixteenth century and early seventeenth, these were closely linked questions. The basis of his discussion is the traditional *jus in bello*, which forbids direct, intended harm to innocent persons and requires avoiding disproportionate harm overall, for either would itself be an injustice. But Suarez goes well beyond this, arguing that an entire commonwealth may be held responsible for repairing an injury done by its prince or some of its inhabitants and using this argument as justification for postwar reparations, requiring only that these not be disproportionate. In this discussion he considers the question of whether a war may be just on both sides. Vitoria before him had argued for what I have called "simultaneous ostensible justice," the possibility that both sides could, because of invincible ignorance, believe themselves in the right, and no one but God could know which, if either, was right. Suarez takes a harder line, consistent with his conception that there is just cause for war only in response to some grave fault, though he does admit, in language that echoes Vitoria's, that "cases of ignorance" may arise in which the war appears just on both sides.[65]

On the principal questions with which the present book is concerned, those of the nature of sovereignty and the shift toward emphasizing defense as the principal just cause for war, Suarez holds more closely to the main line of the earlier just war tradition than most other writers on just war during the sixteenth and early seventeenth centuries. Their trend in thinking pointed toward what came to be the new norm. While Suarez's careful analysis and argument serve as a reminder of how the new conditions of international politics and warfare could be addressed without moving so far in this new direction, for his contemporaries this was not enough.

Notes

1. *Summa theologiae*, II/II, Q. 40; citations are from www.newadvent.org /summa/3040.htm.
2. Augustine, *Questiones in heptateuchum*, q. x, *super Josue*.
3. Gratian, *Decretum*, Part II, causa 23, Q. 2, canon 1; Gregory Reichberg, Henrik Syse, and Endre Begby, eds., *Ethics of War*, 113.
4. *Summa theologiae* II/II, Q. 40, A. 1; Reichberg, Syse, and Begby, *Ethics of War*, 177.
5. Aquinas, *Summa theologiae* II/II, Q. 42, A. 2, Reply Obj. 3; Reichberg, Syse, and Begby, *Ethics of War*, 187.
6. John Calvin, *Institutes of the Christian Religion* 2:657.
7. A. P. D'Entreves, ed., *Aquinas: Selected Political Writings* (Oxford: Basil Blackwell, 1965), 3–83.
8. Born, *The Education of a Christian Prince by Desiderius Erasmus*.
9. Gewirth, *Marsilius of Padua*.
10. Alighieri, *De monarchia*.
11. Vanderpol, *La doctrine scolastique du droit de guerre*, 250.
12. Contamine, *War in the Middle Ages*, 271ff.
13. Citations are from D'Entreves, *Aquinas*, 183, 185.
14. Aquinas, *Summa theologiae* II/II, Q. 42, A. 2, Reply Obj. 3; Reichberg, Syse, and Begby, *Ethics of War*, 186.
15. *Summa theologiae* I, Q. 96, A. 4; D'Entreves, *Aquinas*, 105.

16. *Summa theologiae* I, Q. 103, A. 3; D'Entreves, *Aquinas*, 107.
17. *Summa theologiae* I/II, Q. 103, A. 3, I answer that; D'Entreves, *Aquinas*, 109.
18. *Summa theologiae* I/II, Q. 90, A. 3; D'Entreves, *Aquinas*, 111.
19. *Summa theologiae* I/II, Q. 105, A. 1; D'Entreves, *Aquinas*, 149.
20. *Summa theologiae* II/II, Q. 58, A. 1; D'Entreves, *Aquinas*, 165.
21. D'Entreves, *Aquinas*, xiii–xiv.
22. *On Princely Government*, Book One, Chapter II; D'Entreves, *Aquinas*, 11.
23. D'Entreves, *Aquinas*, 13.
24. For example, Chapter IV; D'Entreves, *Aquinas*, 21–23.
25. Chapter III; D'Entreves, *Aquinas*, 15.
26. Chapter VII; D'Entreves, *Aquinas*, 37.
27. Ibid.
28. Chapter VI; D'Entreves, *Aquinas*, 29.
29. Ibid.
30. Article 2, I answer that; Reichberg, Syse, and Begby, *Ethics of War*, 194.
31. Ibid.
32. Article 2, I answer that; Reichberg, Syse, and Begby, *Ethics of War*, 195.
33. Reply Obj. 3; Reichberg, Syse, and Begby, *Ethics of War*, 186.
34. Chapter 6; D'Entreves, *Aquinas*, 31.
35. Chapter 6; D'Entreves, *Aquinas*, 33.
36. Cajetan, Commentary to *Summa theologiae* II–II, q. 40, a. 1; Reichberg, Syse, and Begby, *Ethics of War*, 243–44.
37. Reichberg, Syse, and Begby, *Ethics of War*, 150–51.
38. Ibid., 242.
39. Ibid., 244.
40. Ibid., 245.
41. See also Johnson, *Just War Tradition and the Restraint of War*, 172–89.
42. *De jure belli*, Q. 1, A. 2; Reichberg, Syse, and Begby, *Ethics of War*, 311–13.
43. Ibid.
44. *De jure belli*, Q. 1, A. 1: Reichberg, Syse, and Begby, *Ethics of War*, 309.
45. *De jure belli*, Q. 1, A. 2.3; Reichberg, Syse, and Begby, *Ethics of War*, 312.
46. Ibid.
47. Ibid.
48. Hamilton, *Political Thought in Sixteenth-Century Spain*, 160.
49. Dawson, *Religion and the Rise of Western Culture*, 143.
50. Ibid., 172.
51. Huizinga, *The Waning of the Middle Ages*, 49.
52. *De jure belli* Q. 1, A. 2.3; Reichberg, Syse, and Begby, *Ethics of War*, 313.
53. *De jure belli* Q. 1, A. 3; Reichberg, Syse, and Begby, *Ethics of War*, 313–14.
54. *De jure belli* Q.2, A. 1.1, A. 2.3; Reichberg, Syse, and Begby, *Ethics of War*, 318–19.

55. *De bello*, Section II.1: Reichberg, Syse, and Begby, *Ethics of War*, 343.
56. *De bello*, Section II.1; Reichberg, Syse, and Begby, *Ethics of War*, 344.
57. *De bello*, Section II.2; Reichberg, Syse, and Begby, *Ethics of War*, 344–45.
58. *De bello*, Section II.4; Reichberg, Syse, and Begby, *Ethics of War*, 345.
59. *De bello*, Section IV.1; Reichberg, Syse, and Begby, *Ethics of War*, 347–48.
60. *De indis*, Q. 3; Reichberg, Syse, and Begby, *Ethics of War*, 300–304.
61. *De bello*, Section IV.5; Reichberg, Syse, and Begby, *Ethics of War*, 349.
62. *De bello*, Section V.1–6; Reichberg, Syse, and Begby, *Ethics of War*, 353–55.
63. *De bello*, Section VI.1–6; Reichberg, Syse, and Begby, *Ethics of War*, 357–59.
64. *De bello*, Section VII; Reichberg, Syse, and Begby, *Ethics of War*, 360–68.
65. *De bello*, Section VII.19; Reichberg, Syse, and Begby, *Ethics of War*, 366.

3

Sovereign Authority and the Justified Use of Force in Luther and the Reformation

Martin Luther

The parameters of Luther's thought on war are defined by four of his writings: *Temporal Authority: To What Extent It Should Be Obeyed* (1523),[1] *Against the Robbing and Murdering Hordes of Peasants* (1525),[2] *Whether Soldiers, Too, Can Be Saved* (1526),[3] and *On War against the Turk* (1529).[4] Perhaps most people who know anything at all about Luther on war know him through his treatise against the peasants, which one standard collection excerpts under the title "Stab, Smite, Slay."[5] But this is the wrong place to begin. The best beginning point is the earliest and most fundamental of the writings named above, *Temporal Authority*. This work establishes the general framework of Luther's political theory around the concept of the two "kingdoms" (that of God and that of the world) with their respective "governments" (the spiritual and the temporal or secular). This is the proper place to begin to examine Luther's thought on war, because, along with the mainstream of just war tradition he inherited and employed, for Luther the question of authority is the most fundamental one for use of the sword. So it is here that we begin.

The distinction between the spiritual and the temporal was passed on to Luther and his contemporaries as part of their common intellectual heritage from the Middle Ages, though Luther and his papalist adversaries interpreted the meaning of the distinction in sharply different ways. The papalists of the previous century and of Luther's own time held that the spiritual authority not only has its own exclusive sphere in the world but also occupies a place of superiority over the secular within the world. On this view the papacy could create and depose rulers or discipline them as needed. Further, the papacy itself (though not subordinate bishops and clergy) possessed authority for use of the sword, both for specifically religious purposes (to protect true religion and to punish dissent and heresy), and for secular purposes (to oppose temporal rulers judged guilty of misgovernment), especially if that was manifest in opposition to the true religion of the Catholic Church. This was the so-called two swords doctrine: that power of the sword belongs to the papacy as well as to the highest temporal authorities. Based on an allegorical reading of Luke 22:38 ("And they said, Lord, here are two swords. And he said unto them, It is enough" [RSV]), this theory justified military coercion on the part of the Church and even the pope's direct command of military forces for this purpose.

Luther, opposing this papalist construct of authority, argued that, properly understood, the spiritual and secular or temporal authorities occupy their own realms: that neither has authority over the other outside its own realm, and that within each other's realm each is subordinate to the other. In the "kingdom" of the world, then, rightful authority belongs to the secular powers, extending even to their regulation of religious matters. This follows, Luther argued, from the divine institution of government at the beginning of time. Likewise, in the "kingdom" of God spiritual authority is supreme; yet this does not extend to any authority over worldly government. Every Christian, for Luther, is a citizen of both realms but has different responsibilities and owes different allegiances in each. The dialectic tension that this conception establishes is intensified by his picture of the world as a disorderly, sinful state of being in which the responsibility of the secular government includes the duty of using force to punish those who are evil and to protect the righteous. This duty of the worldly authorities gives them the power of the sword. But there is no power corresponding to this in the godly kingdom, where evil is to be combated not by the sword but by the Gospel. Nor, because of the separation between the two realms, do the spiritual authorities have any command over the secular authorities in their use of the sword. This is, in brief, the "one sword" position.

Protestant commentary on this dispute has generally tended to render it as establishing a fundamental difference between Catholic political thought and that of the Reformation. While this interpretation certainly fits the dispute as it played out during the era of the Reformation, it misses a great deal of the larger picture. In fact, the "one sword"–"two swords" argument (using the terminology of the Reformation era) or the dispute over the relative extent of temporal and churchly authority (in the terms of the broader debate) had already been engaged in the canonical writings of the twelfth and thirteenth centuries, where the language of the debate was remarkably like that reflected in Luther's own discussion. The canonists in question, Gratian's two waves of successors, the Decretists and the Decretalists, approached the matter through specific attention to the question of authority for just war. Did the pope have it, as the Vicar of Christ on earth, and if so, did subordinate archbishops and bishops have it? Their answer to the latter was explicitly no: The right of the sword is denied to archbishops, bishops, and any other clergy and religious, and none of these may bear arms or fight in war for any reason. This is the position reflected in Aquinas's answer to the question of whether clergy may take part in war: "Warlike pursuits are altogether incompatible with the duties of a bishop and a cleric."[6] By the time he wrote, this was a settled issue. The case of the pope was slightly different; over several decades of debate the canonists gradually defined a more and more restricted right for the pope to authorize war. By the end of this period of development of canon law, that right was limited to the case of crusades, and even there it did not extend to the actual command of troops. Although only the pope could authorize a crusade, he could not be a general in it; the command of troops was reserved for persons in secular positions of authority. But giving the pope authority to initiate crusades implicitly imposed a restriction on the secular authorities: It meant that they could not authorize war for religion. So what of authority for use of the sword, for authorizing a just war, in all cases other than a crusade? The canonists agreed on this fairly early, in their effort to deny *duellum* (private use of the sword) while allowing *bellum* (use of the sword on public authority to serve the public good): Only those temporal authorities with no temporal superior have such a right. This meant in practice that only kings, the emperor, and princes of traditionally independent states could justly authorize just war. Anyone who had a temporal superior to whom he could turn for adjudication of disputes does not, the canonists agreed, possess the necessary authority to initiate such use of armed force. Again, this was a settled matter by the time of Aquinas, and it is reflected in his position on just war. In short, using the language of the Reformation era, the canonists' answer was essentially the "one-sword" position, but with the single exception of the pope's right to authorize crusades, which would then be fought by secular authorities with the forces under their commands.

This thirteenth-century resolution of the question of who possesses the authority necessary to wage just war effectively reserved that authority for temporal sovereigns, but left one small crack in the door for the supreme spiritual authority, the pope, to authorize resort to the sword: the case of the crusades. In the fifteenth century, in the context of the struggle for power between the popes and the Holy Roman emperors, supporters of the papacy in this struggle widened the crack by arguing that the popes had the necessary authority to use arms against the emperors. The device they employed was to argue for excommunication or another form of ecclesiastical discipline against the emperors and their supporters, and thus to declare them to be in the position of heretics or unbelievers; then the pope could authorize the use of force against them as a manifestation of his right to authorize crusades. It is here that the two-swords idea as confronted by Luther and the other Reformers first gained strength. It is safe to say that the canonists of the twelfth and thirteenth centuries did not anticipate such a manipulation of their conclusions. But in any case, the papalist arguments put forward in the context of the struggle between the papacy and the empire, once established there, were easily turned against the Reformers and their supporters in the next century. Luther's advocacy of the one-sword position was in fact in line with the conclusion that was reached by the canonists in the thirteenth century and reflected in Aquinas's understanding of authority for just war. The two-swords position, while strong enough in theory and in political power to inflame the wars of religion of the Reformation era, was never in fact deeply rooted in Christian doctrine or law, and after the end of those religious wars it disappeared. No pope for more than three centuries has claimed the right to authorize the force of arms in the name of religion. So Luther's position on the nature of authority for the sword, though the focus of controversy in his own time, was in fact the more orthodox, in terms of both its antecedents and the subsequent history of Catholic doctrine.

To put this a different way, the one-sword doctrine reveals Luther's acceptance of the main line of just war thinking, according to which the temporal government alone possesses the sovereign authority to employ military force in terms of Romans 13:3–4. For medieval writers and Luther alike, *bellum* meant the prince's use of force against both the external and the internal enemies of the order, justice, and peace of the political community. Government has the dual obligation to ensure justice and peace for its citizens and to ensure their protection against violence and injustice imposed by others.

While Aquinas derived the right to authorize war and to use force in a just cause from the natural order as well as from Romans 13, Luther, with his reliance on "scripture alone" (*sola scriptura*), focused on Paul and interpreted the allowance of force in terms of the broader theological standard of Christian love, as exemplified in this observation from *On War against the Turk*: "It is . . . a work of Christian love to protect and defend a whole community with the sword and not let the people be abused."[7] In this way he, like Aquinas, connected just cause to the authority necessary for war; only here this cause is described as "a work of Christian love" and not as an obligation of governing itself (though in other contexts, as we shall see in a moment, Luther spoke of this obligation as having to do with the "office" of temporal authority). Also like Aquinas, and within the broad frame of the Augustinian tradition on just use of armed force, Luther linked authority to war to the aim of peace, as in this passage from *Whether Soldiers, Too, Can Be Saved?* where Luther employs language very much like that of Augustine which Aquinas quoted in explaining the end of peace: Luther writes, "What else is war but the punishment of wrong and evil? Why does anyone go to war except because he desires peace and obedience?"[8] In this treatise Luther specifically addresses the question of whether Christians should accept military service. His answer is not only that the Christian should not avoid military service, but that such service is a duty for him, as a way of contributing to order, peace, and justice in the kingdom of this world. For the private Christian individual, that is, this is a part of his good citizenship: "Every lord and prince is bound to protect his people and to preserve the peace for them. That is his office; that is why he has the sword, Romans 13[:4]. This should be a matter of conscience for him. And he should on this basis be certain that the work is right in the eyes of God and commanded by him."[9]

"Bound to protect his people and to preserve the peace for them." It is the prince's "office," but it should also be "a matter of conscience for him." This is similar language to what Luther used the previous year in *Against the Robbing and Murdering Hordes of Peasants*: "If [the ruler] does not fulfill the duties of his office by punishing some and protecting others, he commits as great a sin before God as when someone who has not been given the sword commits murder [the latter a reference, in this case, to the rebellious peasants]. If he is able to punish and does not do it . . . he becomes guilty of all the murder and evil these people commit."[10] And a bit later, "The rulers have a good conscience and a just cause; they can, therefore, say to God with all confidence of heart, 'Behold, my God, . . . you have given me the sword to use against evildoers (Romans 13[:4]).'" By contrast, the peasants have no such right of the sword; their killing is murder, their collective action in arms not just war but rebellion and revolution: Theirs is "a bad conscience and an unjust cause." But what can Luther have meant by this last judgment? After all, we know from his *Admonition to Peace* that he was in sympathy with many of the peasants' grievances.[11] How, then, can they have an "unjust cause"? This points us back to the importance of the requirement of sovereign authority as understood in the normative just war tradition: The sovereign, as the one responsible for an order that serves justice and peace, is the one who must judge whether a just cause exists in a given case, just as he is the one who must, if he decides to use armed force, do so with right intention (or as Luther puts it, a "good conscience"). No one not in the sovereign's position, finally, is able to do this. Advice from others should be solicited, but in the end the sovereign's right to use force comes from his responsibility for the order, justice, and peace of the entire community. The peasants are not in that situation; their resort to arms can only be unjust, disorderly, destructive of peace, an act of wrong intention ("bad conscience," as Luther puts it). So the question of authority for Luther (as for the broader just war tradition) is the central one where use of the sword is concerned. Only from the perspective of sovereign authority can the justice of the cause be determined and the right intention maintained.

But what if the ruler is manifestly a bad ruler? What if he has neglected or flouted his responsibilities for the common good or has used his power to do manifest evil? The answer cannot be armed resistance, because persons not in sovereign authority cannot justly take the sword on their own authority. For Luther such persons, private individuals, have only three options: They may disobey and accept punishment, flee to another political community and accept its authority, or, if uncertain as to the justice or injustice of their ruler's government, "obey without peril to their souls."[12] For the ruler's part, his fate is in God's hands. But it is also, under the proper circumstances, in the hands of others in positions of sovereign temporal authority, whose own obligation to punish evil and support good may extend to war against the evildoer, his punishment, and his deposition, an argument similar to what we have already encountered in Aquinas. "Regime change" is thus not a new idea, but one found in the conception of sovereign authority for just war, and rooted in the notion of sovereign responsibility for promoting the good and punishing evildoers.

Windows on Later Reformation Thought: Calvin, Althusius, Gentili, Ames

An examination of Luther's thinking is an essential first step to understanding how the Reformation dealt with the concept of sovereignty. In important respects Luther's treatment of sovereignty reflected the assumptions he inherited from medieval thought and practice, though the stresses that challenged these assumptions are also visible in his thought. Later Protestant thinkers increasingly replaced the medieval assumptions with new conceptions, contributing to an intellectual transformation that reshaped the idea of sovereignty. The following discussion examines the contributions of four of the most important of these later Protestant thinkers in this transformation.

Shifts in the Context

The central elements in Luther's thinking about sovereign authority and the use of armed force—inherited, as the above discussion shows, from earlier Christian canonical and theological thought on just war—also appear in other Protestant treatments of these subjects in Luther's own time and afterward. Yet the shifting historical conditions of the sixteenth century also inevitably affected how Protestant thinkers dealt with the topics of sovereignty and the use of armed force, laying the groundwork for later thinking that departed more and more from the assumptions and norms found in the inherited tradition.

At the very core of the classic conception of just war was the conception of sovereign rule in terms of responsibility for the common good, a responsibility that might require the use of armed force to ensure the order, justice, and peace of the political community. So long as there was general agreement as to religion, religious norms and sanctions could be appealed to, along with the norms of natural law, to define the order, justice, and peace that it was the sovereign's duty to serve. Yet when this agreement disappeared, as it did beginning with the onset of the Reformation's challenge to Catholicism, the conception of the role of the sovereign relative to religion necessarily shifted. On the inherited assumption, the sovereign's responsibility included the use of secular authority and power to maintain right religion as an element in public order; now it also became the sovereign's responsibility to determine what was to be right religion in his domain. This new conception took legal form in the doctrine of *cuius regio, eius religio* (to whom the domain, to him the religion), which became the law of the German Empire after the Peace of Augsburg ended the first round of post-Reformation religious warfare between Protestants and Catholics. This formulation had the immediate positive effect of providing a basis for ending the armed conflict among the states of the empire, but it also implicitly opened the door to a sixteenth-century version of the idea of holy war by making the establishment of one or another form of religion a political aim. So far as the conception of sovereignty was concerned, this had two opposite implications. On the one hand, its way of linking the transcendent (religion) to the immanent (the political sphere) tended to absolutize the role of the sovereign as the arbiter of how his society should relate to the transcendent. The conceptions of sovereignty given voice by later theorists like Bodin and Hobbes rested on this earlier development. But there was a second implication that was the opposite of this: If the sovereign did not establish right religion, as this was understood by some or all the populace of the sovereign's political community, they might invoke the cause of religion as justification for replacing their ruler with one who supported what they understood to be right religion. The interplay between these two opposite implications worked against any solution to religious conflict that involved the toleration of religious difference; that is, they both tended to inflame conflict over religion. The solution, finally, was to find ways to take religion out of the political picture as thoroughly as possible. The first major step in this direction, given form in the Peace of Westphalia, which ended the last of the great post-Reformation religious wars, redefined sovereignty itself in a way unrelated to what Luther and other Reformation writers called the "office" of the sovereign, which was defined as the sovereign's moral responsibility for the good of the society governed. How much was lost by this shift took considerable time to become apparent; how to recover at least some of what was lost requires a great deal of historical and thematic untangling.

The changing historical conditions of the sixteenth century also included major shifts in the nature of warfare. These shifts followed from two distinct developments: a change in the nature of armies and the use of far more destructive kinds of weapons than had earlier been available. I have discussed these developments in more detail elsewhere and will simply summarize them here.[13] As to the first, the emergence of the modern era saw the end of armies based on knights, who had in the process of becoming knights undergone a long and concerted socialization into the code of chivalric conduct (on the battlefield and off), with increasingly much larger armies of common men, who had not undergone such socialization but instead were governed by military discipline, which was enforced by officers who were themselves members of the chivalric class. The chivalric code had made the exercise of restraint in warfare a matter of personal moral obligation; while the new codes of military discipline attempted to extend such restraints to the new armies of common men, they did not become a matter of personal morality for each soldier, and in the absence of the immediate enforcement of discipline by members of the officer class, these armies tended to ignore the traditional restraints found there, not sparing noncombatants, using disproportionate force, killing prisoners, and so on. The tendencies toward unrestrained warfare introduced by the new armies of common men were aggravated by the introduction of firearms, both personal weapons and field artillery. Any wound from one of these weapons was likely to be lethal because of the infection that followed, which could not be treated with the medical care of the time. Further, the larger guns were inherently indiscriminate when used against targets that included noncombatants as well as combatants. It became seductively easy to use such weapons to destroy noncombatant property and lives as a way of getting at the enemy combatants, rather than taking care to aim at the combatants in such a way as to try to spare the noncombatants and their property.

In the context of the newly unrestrained and more highly destructive warfare of the sixteenth century, the limits on conduct in war that had loomed large as late as the Hundred Years' War were stretched and often effectively disappeared. What this meant for the exercise of sovereign responsibility relative to the use of armed force was that more emphasis was placed on the decision whether or not to use such force in the first place (what later legal writers would term the *jus ad bellum*) and less on restraints on conduct in war (the *jus in bello*). This affected how Reformation-era writers thought about the sovereign's use of armed force in exercising responsibility for the common good. Ultimately, in the thought of Grotius and after, a reverse movement set in and quickly triumphed, with a limit on the right to use armed force in the first place and a new emphasis on the observance of restraint in warfare once it began.

Now to some particular examples of thinkers in which the influence of one or more of these developments appear. I will briefly discuss two major Continental thinkers from the Reformed tradition, the theologians John Calvin (1509–64) and Johannes Althusius (1557–1638), and two writers from the context of the English Reformation who wrote specifically about just war, the Italian Protestant Alberico Gentili (1552–1608) and the Puritan theologian William Ames (1576–1633).

John Calvin

Early in his theological masterwork, *Institutes of the Christian Religion*, Calvin distinguished two kinds of human government, the spiritual and civil rule. The exercise of the former belongs to the church, that of the latter to the civil authorities. Most of the *Institutes* is given over to exploring the proper dimensions of the former, developed through a close engagement with the Bible; he does not turn to the latter until the very end of this work, devoting its final chapter (Book IV, Chapter XX) to the subject of civil government. Such government is necessary, its use being "not less than that of bread and water, light and air, while its dignity is more excellent."[14] He goes on in more detail:

> Its object is not merely, like those things, to enable men to breathe, eat, drink, and be warmed (though it certainly includes all these, while it enables them to live together); [but its object is also] that no idolatry, no blasphemies against the name of God, no calumnies against his truth, nor other offences to religion, break out and be disseminated among the people; that the public quiet be not disturbed, that every man's property be kept secure, that men may carry on innocent commerce with each other, that honesty and modesty be cultivated; in short, that a public form of religion may exist among Christians, and humanity among men.[15]

Calvin defines "the whole order of civil government" as having three parts: "The Magistrate, who is president and guardian of the laws; the Laws, according to which he governs; and the People, who are governed by the laws, and obey the magistrate."[16] His use of the term "magistrate" for the secular ruler recalls the medieval canonical description of the sovereign as a judge in deciding the justice of the use of armed force; yet for Calvin, government as the exercise of a kind of judicial wisdom extends across the whole of the operations of civil society. But the term "magistrate" also refers to the Latin word *magister*, "teacher"; so for Calvin the magistrate is one who teaches the people what is required for a good life together.

Just a bit later he introduces a demanding further characterization: As "viceregents of God," those holding magisterial authority must seek to "exhibit a kind of image of the Divine providence, guardianship, goodness, benevolence, and justice."[17]

Exactly how these high goals are to be met is indicated by Calvin's comments on what he takes to be the three options for the exercise of civil government: monarchy, aristocracy, and "popular ascendancy." Despite the prevalence of monarchical rule, he observes that monarchy "is prone to tyranny." In societies ruled by popular ascendancy, "there is the strongest tendency to sedition." Though in aristocratic government there is a tendency toward factionalism, for Calvin this is outweighed by other considerations: "Owing . . . to the vices or defects of men, it is safer and more tolerable when several bear rule, that they may thus mutually assist, instruct, and admonish each other," and so that the group may curb any tendency to excess by any one of them.[18]

Civil rule, then, the exercise of sovereignty in a civil community, is described here fundamentally in terms of moral responsibility on the part of those wielding governing authority. This is the older tradition restated in a way that emphasizes the obligation for persons bearing such authority to adhere to definite standards, while subject to the restraint of others if they stray from adherence to those standards.

On the specific subject of the use of armed force, Calvin adheres to the basic frame of the just war tradition before him, but he also makes some shifts in line with the changing context. He is squarely with the tradition in locating the justification for the use of armed force in the responsibilities of sovereignty: "It is sometimes necessary for kings and states to take up arms in order to undertake public vengeance," he writes; and again, "Natural equity and duty . . . demand that princes be armed not only to repress private crimes by judicial inflictions, but to defend the subjects committed to their guardianship when they are hostilely assailed."[19] Sovereigns are to employ armed force, "not for their own advantage, but for the good and service of others."[20] But the same doubtfulness—about "the vices and defects of men"—that leads Calvin to prefer autocratic forms of the exercise of government over monarchy leads him to emphasize defense and common action when thinking of the threats that may be encountered. Thus he writes as follows: "On this right of war depends the right of garrisons, leagues, and other civil munitions. By garrisons, I mean those which are stationed in states for the defence of the frontiers; by leagues, the alliances which are made by neighbouring princes, on the ground that if any disturbance arise within their territories, they will mutually assist each other, and combine their forces to repel the common enemies of the human race; under civil munitions, I include everything pertaining to the military art."[21] Another shift is that for Calvin the role of government is a kind of trusteeship for the whole people of the society. This is a theme that also appears in other authors from this period who write on this topic, and it prepares the way for the shift in the whole idea of sovereignty reached in Grotius's thought, in which sovereignty is a quality of the society rather than a moral responsibility of the ruler or rulers. Calvin makes this point in two ways: by emphasizing that the revenues available to those who govern are "not so much private chests as treasuries of the whole people,"[22] and by stressing the importance of the society's laws, which the magistrate serves by governing.[23]

Johannes Althusius

Johannes Althusius was a Calvinist legal and theological thinker who spent the last thirty-four years of his life as a "magistrate," "managing public affairs in the German city of Emden in much the same way as Calvin had in Geneva."[24] Born forty-eight years after Calvin, Althusius was an older contemporary of Grotius. In his thinking on government, the concept of sovereignty has clearly and decisively moved away from its earlier locus in the personal moral responsibility of the ruler to what he called the *populus*. This was "an organic assemblage of various capacities: families, guilds, corporations, cities, provinces, and commonwealths."[25] Althusius describes the use of armed force as belonging to the part of the "special right of sovereignty" that "pertains to the protection of the universal association and symbiosis."[26] "It consists," he writes, "first, in defense, and then, in the care of goods belonging to the universal association."[27] Defense, for him, is the basis of just cause for war, which may be waged only "when all other remedies have first been exhausted and peace or justice cannot otherwise be obtained."[28] With this as a basis,

Althusius goes on to distinguish seven forms of just cause: "the recovery of things taken away through violence by another people"; "defense against violence inflicted by another, and the repulsion of it"; "the necessity for preserving liberty, privileges, rights, peace, and tranquility, and for defending true religion"; "when a foreign people deny peaceful transit through its province without good reason"; "when subjects rise up against their prince and lord . . . though they have been admonished many times"; "when any prince, lord, or city has so contemptuously and repeatedly scorned the decisions of courts that justice cannot otherwise be administered and defended"; and "when agreements are not implemented by the other party, when he does not keep his promises, and when tyranny is practiced upon subjects."[29] This is an interesting list, both reflecting classic just war tradition and going beyond it. A close look at the seven specific forms of just cause shows that not all are defensive in the narrow sense that already appears in Calvin and later becomes the norm: protection of the society's territory against armed attack by another. Althusius's third form of just cause anticipates Grotius's emphasis on the defense of the "ancient rights and privileges" of the people without specifically attaching this to the defense of territorial borders. There is an internal tension between the fifth and sixth forms of just cause, the former reflecting the older emphasis on the need for order above all and the latter reflecting Calvin's idea that some governing authorities may rightly be disciplined by others. Finally, Althusius's final form of just cause, while reflecting the idea already found in Aquinas that sovereigns may oppose tyranny by force, is stated more explicitly than was the earlier norm; it opens the door to a first use of armed force against other societies on the grounds that their people are being unjustly governed.

Later Althusius discusses these matters using slightly different language, emphasizing the authority necessary:

> A just cause of war is one that depends upon both right and the authority of the supreme magistrate. . . . These causes can easily be reduced to two, the first of which is defense and the other vindication. The former repulses and the latter vindicates injury launched against God, the commonwealth, its subjects, or the church. . . . The authority of the supreme magistrate in undertaking war, and the agreement of the orders of the realm, are so necessary for the waging of war that without them a war is said to be unjustly and unlawfully undertaken.[30]

But under two conditions, Althusius goes on, an "inferior magistrate" may undertake war: to defend himself and his subjects against an unjust "violent invasion," or when the superior magistrate "does not do his duty, or exercises tyranny over his subjects." This leads him to a more detailed examination of the justice of resistance to tyranny.[31] His definition of tyranny clearly reflects concern for the divisions over right religion that had not yet been resolved in European culture: "violat[ing] the worship of God and assault[ing] the rights and foundations of the commonwealth." When this takes place by the use of armed force, then the ruler may be opposed by armed force from both inside the realm and outside it. Like Calvin, Althusius holds that within the society this opposition must be authorized and led by "public persons"; private citizens, who "do not have the use and right of the sword," may participate in the force led by such persons, but without such an authorized resistance, they should normally avoid obeying the tyrant by fleeing his jurisdiction. Yet Althusius identifies an important exception to this general rule, an exception that moves him some distance from Calvin and Luther before him, and from the earlier just war tradition: If the tyrant uses force against private persons, then "in case of the need to defend their lives resistance is permitted to them . . . by the natural law and the arrangements constituting kings." This exception opens the door rather widely to the individual resort to force, undercutting the earlier consensus that the right to use such force derives from the responsibility of governing. In the context of the Thirty Years' War, which was being waged while Althusius was writing, this was an important exception.

Alberico Gentili

Gentili was not a theologian but a jurist, known especially for his work on the idea of just war. An Italian Protestant, he did his most significant work in England, where he and his family had fled to avoid religious persecution.

Just war, Gentili argues, must be "public and official and there must be princes on both sides to direct the war."[32] That is, just war requires the authorization of the supreme ruler in the society. On this Gentili holds to the standard position established in the earlier just war tradition. But he further argues that for an armed conflict to be war, it must meet this standard on both sides. Since "the violence of private individuals and of brigands" is not war, then neither is the use of armed force against them by public authority. The earlier just war tradition had put the matter differently: *Bellum iustum*, "just war," was the use of armed force on sovereign authority to respond to threats and disturbances to justice and peace, whether posed by persons and groups within the political community or coming from outside that community. Luther, Calvin, and Althusius had held to this conception. The distinction Gentili makes between the use of armed force internal to a society and external, between societies, takes hold and becomes the norm in later thinking and practice. The moral basis for the use of such force by the sovereign authority (the judgment by the person or persons holding such authority that justice or peace is threatened or has been disturbed) tends to get lost when this distinction is not preserved. This happens in Gentili's thought, leading him to a version of the judgment that war may be just on both sides at once. Vitoria was the first to introduce this idea; for him, it did not replace the idea that justice should be on only one side, but followed from invincible ignorance on one or both sides in a war as to the true justice at stake. For Gentili, though, the new norm is presented as a disagreement on justice: "It is the nature of wars for both sides to maintain that they are supporting a just cause. . . . But we for the most part are unacquainted with that truth. Therefore we aim at justice as it appears from man's standpoint. . . . If it is doubtful on which side justice is, and if each side aims at justice, neither can be called unjust."[33] This leads Gentili to the same conclusion reached before him by Vitoria: Whatever one side thinks of its own justice or injustice and that of the enemy, even when the "injustice is clearly evident on one of the two sides," the rights of war apply to both sides equally, and each side is to abide by them in their conduct toward the other.[34] This is the position also taken by Grotius. It marks a shift in emphasis in just war thinking away from the justice of taking up arms (*jus ad bellum*), which had been the central focus of classic just war thought and remained so right through the sixteenth century (as we see in both Luther and Calvin, who do not have any notion of a possibility of justice on both sides in a conflict at once), toward a new stress on right conduct (the *jus in bello*, or "law of war"), which becomes the dominating feature in modern thinking and practice. On the matter of authority for war, while, as Gentili insists, the authority of the sovereign is still necessary, the conception of the sovereign is as a judge of right and wrong. It is a relatively small step to the position staked out by Grotius, in which the role of the ruling authority is fundamentally responsive, with the matter of justice or injustice being redefined in terms of the violation of a political community's borders by armed attack. This, of course, is the position ultimately made part of positive international law in the Pact of Paris (the Kellogg-Briand Pact) of 1928 and chapter 2 of the United Nations Charter.

In sharp contrast to what we have seen in both Calvin and Althusius, Gentili explicitly rules out war for religion: "A thing which is a matter of choice should not be made a necessity."[35] He goes on to suggest that appeal to religion serves to mask other reasons, rooted in "nature," for enmity and conflict: "War is not waged on account of religion, and war is not natural either with others or even with the Turks. But we have war with the Turks because they act as our enemies, plot against us, and threaten us."[36] In the language of the present world, Gentili would count as a realist.

I have stressed how Gentili opens the way to positions adopted and furthered by Grotius, positions that become the norm in later modernity. This is also the case with Gentili's discussion of defense as just cause, both because of his stress on the justice of fighting in defense and because of his extension of the idea of acting in defense to include acting before an actual attack: "One ought to provide not only against an offence which is being committed, but also against one which may possibly be committed. Force must be repelled and kept aloof by force."[37] This allowance puts a closer focus on defense as the central just cause, making the use of force for other reasons in effect threats that need to be preemptively defended against.

William Ames

The English Puritan theologian William Ames studied at Christ's College, Cambridge, where his tutor was the eminent Puritan divine William Perkins. Ames spent the majority of his working life in Holland, where he produced his two major works, *Conscience, with the Power and Cases Thereof* and *Medulla Theologiae*, both of which were considered essential to Puritan libraries in both England and New England.[38] His residence in Holland provided a close perspective on the Thirty Years' War and involved him deeply in the intellectual discussions that swirled in that country over both theology and politics, discussions that also influenced Grotius. His theology was scrupulously Calvinist, but his style was close to the scholastic, and particularly in his discussion of just war and the question of sovereignty, which appears in *Conscience*, he shows the influence not only of Gratian and Thomas Aquinas but of the Spanish Neo-Scholastics, especially Vitoria; yet he takes the idea of just war and its component ideas in his own direction.

"What conditions are required to make a War lawfull?" Ames asks, responding with four criteria: just cause, just authority, right intention, and just manner of waging.[39] The first three correspond to the listing given by Thomas Aquinas, though Ames changes the order of the first two and describes their content somewhat differently; the last criterion is a capsule reference to the *jus in bello*, which in general gained in emphasis during the whole period of the religious wars of the Reformation era.

But in the present context our first concern is how Ames treats the matter of authority for a just war. He writes as follows: "In the second place is required just authority. Now such an authority though in respect of a defensive Warre is to bee found in every Common-wealth although imperfect; because all men have authority by the Law of nature, to defend themselves and to repell force by force, yet in respect of an assaulting Warre, it is not, but in the power of a perfect Commonwealth, which does not depend nor has any recourse to a superiour, but is in all things sufficient it selfe and entire in every point, which is requisite to a due Government."[40]

This is not Aquinas's language but that of Vitoria in his *De jure belli*, Question 1, Article 2,[41] where the same distinctions appear between perfect and imperfect political communities and between the right to offensive war and that to defensive war only. Vitoria's position on this has been discussed more fully in chapter 2, but to summarize, there are two main issues at stake.

First, the distinction between perfect and imperfect commonwealths in regard to the use of armed force was essentially made already by the medieval canonists who first defined the shape of a coherent idea of just war: Only rulers with no political superior may undertake war to redress wrongs done and punish evildoing, but anyone has, by nature, the right to use armed force in defense against an attack. Innocent IV had put the matter this way: "It is permissible for anyone to wage war in self-defense or to protect property. Nor is this properly called 'war' (*bellum*), but rather 'defense' (*defensio*)."[42] That is, Innocent and the other canonists of his period wanted to reserve the term *bellum*, "war" properly speaking, for the use of armed force by a ruler with no temporal superior, a sovereign ruler. Such war could be just or unjust, depending on whether the other two criteria, just cause and right intention, were satisfied. This is the usage found in Thomas Aquinas's systematic summary of the doctrine of his time in his question "On War." By Vitoria's period, the term "war" was being used for both sorts of use of force, defensive and offensive, by both sorts of actors, sovereign and not. But the essential distinction made earlier still held.

The second issue raised by Ames's use of Vitoria's language leads to a rather different outcome: For Vitoria it is the *commonwealth*—we might rather say the political community—that "has the authority to declare and wage war," and the authority of the ruler to do so derives from this.[43] This is a significant change from the earlier tradition, locating sovereignty in the community as a whole and describing the ruler as "the authorized representative of the commonwealth."

Now, also before Ames, Calvin had argued something similar, as noted above: The rulership of a political community is a kind of trusteeship for the community as a whole. As I observed when treating this idea as it occurs in Calvin, it is found frequently among writers of this period, whichever side of the religious disputes they were on; though Ames was using the specific language of Vitoria, this was not in tension with his broader theological dependence on Calvin.

The meaning of sovereignty, then, in Ames's thought has become something different from the earlier idea that associated sovereignty directly with the ruler of a political community. There its essence was the exercise of moral responsibility for that community, responsibility not different from the paternal responsibility a father has for his family. The new understanding of sovereignty, though, associates it with the community itself, and the ruler's role is as an agent of that sovereignty on behalf of the community. To be sure, the ruler still has a moral responsibility, but it is to be a faithful agent, not to care for the community as a parent might care for his family. So far as there is still a moral component to sovereignty itself, it has to be found in the members of the community as a whole, and thus it is at once diffuse and abstracted from any individual person's behavior.

English Puritan thought more generally had earlier defined the relation between ruler and those governed in terms of covenant, building on the Old Testament covenant between God and Israel. On this conception each of the parties to the covenant has specific responsibilities, but there is no doubt as to where the superior power and authority are located: in God, the author of the covenant with humanity, and in the ruler. Depending on how the relationship between ruler and people ruled is understood, one may move in the direction of Hobbes's Leviathan or Locke's conception of the social contract. Ames seems to be on the latter side in this, though it is not entirely clear, as it is not clear in Calvin's own thinking.

For the purposes of the questions being examined in the present book, though, the shift in the idea and the location of sovereignty seen in similar ways in Calvin, Vitoria, and Ames points toward making the political community as a whole responsible for its protection and its prosperity, and this, I suggest, helps to explain the move in just war thought during this period toward emphasizing defense as the central justifying cause for resort to armed force on behalf of, by, and for the community: on behalf of, in the actions of the executive ruler; by, in the sense that the entire community, and not only the ruler's own private army, is involved; and for, in the sense that this is the community's effort to correct a threat to itself. Loose ends remain in Ames about this, as in Vitoria and Calvin before him; those loose ends get tied together in a persuasive way in Grotius's work.

Notes

1. Luther, *Works*, vol. 45.
2. Luther, *Works*, vol. 46.
3. Ibid.
4. Ibid.
5. Manschrek, *A History of Christianity*, vol 2., 37–38.
6. *Summa theologiae* II/II, Q. 40, A. 2.
7. Luther, *Works*, 46:121.
8. Ibid., 46:95; cf. Aquinas, *Summa theologiae* II/II, Q. 40, A. 1.
9. Luther, *Works*, 46:121.
10. Ibid., 46:53.
11. Ibid., 46:3–43.
12. Ibid., 45:126.
13. Johnson, *Just War Tradition and the Restraint of War*, 172–89.
14. IV.XX.3; Calvin, *Institutes of the Christian Religion*, 2:652.
15. IV.XX.3; Calvin, *Institutes of the Christian Religion*, 2:652–53.
16. IV.XX.3; Ibid., 2:653.
17. IV.XX.6; Calvin, *Institutes of the Christian Religion*, 2:655.

18. IV.XX.8; Calvin, *Institutes of the Christian Religion*, 2:657.
19. IV.XX.11; Calvin, *Institutes of the Christian Religion*, 2:661.
20. IV.XX.12; Calvin, *Institutes of the Christian Religion*, 2:662.
21. Ibid.
22. IV.XX.13; Calvin, *Institutes of the Christian Religion*, 2:662.
23. IV.XX.14; Calvin, *Institutes of the Christian Religion*, 2:663.
24. Reichberg, Syse, and Begby, *The Ethics of War*, 378.
25. Ibid.
26. Ibid., 379.
27. Ibid.
28. Ibid.
29. Ibid., 380.
30. Ibid., 381.
31. Ibid., 383–84.
32. Ibid., 373.
33. Ibid., 374.
34. Ibid., 375.
35. Ibid.
36. Ibid., 376.
37. Ibid.
38. Ames, *Conscience, with the Power and Cases Thereof,* (London: n.p, 1639); Ames, *Medulla Theologiae* (London: Robert Allott, 1630).
39. Ames, *Conscience*, Book V, Chapter XXXIII.
40. Ibid., Book V, Chapter XXXIII, Quest. 2.
41. Reichberg, Syse, and Begby, *Ethics of War*, 311–12.
42. Ibid., 150.
43. Ibid., 311–12.

4

Grotius and His Impact:
The Westphalian Settlement, the Idea of the "Law of Nations," and the Emergence of the Territorial Idea of Sovereignty

The Coalescence of a New Way of Thinking in Grotius and His Predecessors

The work of the Spanish Neo-Scholastic theologian Francisco de Vitoria and of the Dutch jurist and philosopher Hugo Grotius mark the beginning and the completion of a shift from medieval to modern understandings of sovereignty, the relations among political communities, and the idea of just war. Both of these men in their thinking reflect the conceptions of the Middle Ages, but both frame new conceptions that became normative for modern political and legal thought after them. Vitoria's work is more directly engaged with the thinking of the Middle Ages, and particularly of Aquinas, on whose conception of just war Vitoria consciously builds his own. Grotius too reflects the medieval inheritance; as Reichberg, Syse, and Begby write in *The Ethics of War*: "Often presented as the founding treatise of the new discipline of international law, [Grotius's] *De iure belli ac pacis* would more accurately be described as a summation of the earlier tradition of just war."[1] But while Grotius certainly depends heavily on the tradition of just war as it had developed before him, he importantly changes the focus, reshapes the content, and gives a new intentionality to the just war idea and its component ideas, and his conception of international law is distinctively different, reflecting his particular way of reading and combining natural law, *jus gentium*, the place of Christian influences, and European thinking and praxis in his own day on the relations among political communities, including war. Grotius's role in securing this redefinition is analogous to that of Thomas Aquinas in the thirteenth century: Aquinas summarized and stated systematically the understandings that had been reached during a long century of canonical debate, from Gratian's *Decretum* through the work of his two generations of successors, the Decretists and the Decretalists; Grotius restated and systematized in the form of a legal conception the new understandings and perspectives that appear in major thinkers of the previous century on just war, from the Catholic Vitoria to the Protestants Gentili, Althusius, and Ames. For the interests of this chapter, the influence of Grotius on subsequent thought and practice is more important than that of Vitoria or any of the other scholars between them, discussed in the previous chapters, who contributed to the transition in political and military thinking from the Middle Ages to the modern. But two elements from earlier thinkers, which Grotius made his own, are important to note explicitly.

First, we should recall how Vitoria reshapes Aquinas's first requirement for *bellum iustum*: the authorization by a prince, a temporal sovereign with no temporal superior. On Aquinas's conception this follows from the responsibility of the sovereign for the commonweal of the political community he rules. This is a conception clearly in line with the twelfth- and thirteenth-century thinking about *ius naturale* as issuing in both rights and responsibilities for political communities and for individuals, including those who govern such communities. But in Vitoria's thinking a shift occurs away from the ruler and to the commonwealth itself. This can be seen in his *De jure belli*, Question 1, Articles 1 and 2. In the former he observes that "the purpose of war is the peace and security of the commonwealth" and then locates the right of war in the commonwealth itself, not in the prince who rules it. Similarly, and more explicitly, in Article 2, he offers as a proposition that "any commonwealth has the authority to declare and wage war," and follows this with another proposition, "in this matter the prince has the same authority as the commonwealth."[2] Here the locus of authority to wage just war is shifted away from the prince to the commonwealth, that is, the political community, and the prince's authority is made dependent on it: As Vitoria comments in connection with the latter proposition, the prince is "the authorized representative of the commonwealth." On this conception sovereignty is defined not as a responsibility of the sovereign as an individual, a duty of rule, but as a right of the community to protect itself. A similar idea, which also reflects the influence of John Calvin, appears as discussed in the previous chapter in the Calvinist theologian Johannes Althusius, a slightly older contemporary of Grotius, where the right of waging war is identified as a right of the *populus*, that is, the people of a commonwealth, though the specific authority for waging war is located in the "supreme magistrate" or, if the supreme magistracy does not act or acts tyrannically, in an "inferior magistrate," acting on behalf of the people.[3]

Both Althusius and Grotius were concerned to define grounds for the use of arms against a sovereign perceived as a tyrant: Specifically, for Grotius, this meant the resistance of the Dutch against the overlordship of the Spanish king (an overlordship that had been won in war) on the grounds that the king had trampled the "ancient rights and privileges" of the Dutch people. The result of such thinking was a new conception of sovereignty as located in the rights of the people of a political community, not as located in the moral responsibility of the ruler of that community. This conception became embodied in the Peace of Westphalia and subsequently became normative for European political theory and practice.

There is a broader story about political theory and behavior under this conceptual regime that might be pursued here, but we will focus specifically on the implications of this shift as seen in the idea of just war, in the conception of natural law, and in the development of a new idea of the law of nations in the thought of Grotius and his successors.

First, as to the idea of just war, the shift in the conception of sovereignty is matched by a shift toward limiting the right to initiate war to cases of defense. Lest the importance of this change be missed, it is important to reflect that medieval thinking had been different. Aquinas does not include defense in his definition of just causes for war, reflecting the position stated flatly by Innocent IV before him that the right to use force in self-defense or to protect one's property is given to all persons in natural law. War (*bellum*, not *defensio*) is different; it is rightly reserved for the prince, who in his authority to uphold the law may retrieve wrongly taken property and punish the evildoer.[4] Thus Aquinas, in his definition of the just war requirement of just cause, quotes Augustine: "A just war is wont to be described as one that avenges wrongs, as when a nation or a state has to be punished, for refusing to make amends for the wrongs inflicted by its subjects, or to restore what it has seized unjustly."[5] As Vanderpol points out, the emphasis in scholastic just war thinking is on serving justice, not on defense.[6] More broadly, as seen in the thinking of Cajetan and Suarez in chapter 2, the justifying cause is vindicative justice: securing justice by setting matters right. So the shift of emphasis to defense is a significant change in understanding what a just war requires.

The traditional conception of just war reasons downward from the moral responsibility of the sovereign ruler to the justification for using armed force; Grotius reasons exactly oppositely, working upward from the justice of individual self-defense to the right of the commonwealth to defend itself by resort to arms. This centrality of the right of defense as the core justification for the use of armed force by a political community becomes a bedrock element of the Westphalian system of international order. In Grotius it is focused in *De iure belli ac pacis*, Book II. Here, in Chapter I.2 Grotius writes, "Three justifiable causes for war are generally cited: defense, recovery of property, and punishment. . . . The first cause of war, then, is an injury, which, even though not actually committed, threatens our persons or property." In the remainder of Book II Grotius focuses on property rights. The result of this way of casting the issues is a clear stress on the idea of defense of property as the first just cause, not only in order of listing, but in priority of importance. He explicitly grounds the right of the use of force by reference back to the right of self-defense (Chapter I.3), a right based on natural law but also guaranteed by the law of nations. Under his pen, the other causes mentioned, the recovery of property and punishment, are justified not by appeals to right or justice, as in the traditional thinking, but by the dominant purpose of defending a nation's territory, and the people who inhabit it, against injury. This is the same kind of reasoning we have encountered in the authors treated in the two previous chapters. Similarly, Grotius connects his understanding of the function of the governing authority of the political community, who in classic just war thinking had represented the good of order and was understood as obligated to act in the service of justice to protect or restore peace, to his emphasis on defense: The prime concern of the person in governing authority should be to protect his nation. In like manner, the security of the nation's territory and people defines the substance of the ideas of justice and peace. It is no great step at all from Grotius's thought to an international system based on the integrity of territorial states, with a formalized conception of war defined according to rules that have to do with protecting and preserving this integrity, and a conception of peace not as the synthesis of order and justice, as in the traditional thinking, but as the absence of war.

On this conception the practical trigger for the justified use of armed force by a political community is a particular kind of injury already done or offered: violation of its territorial borders by another or the threat of immediate violation. Whereas private persons may take arms only in defense of oneself or one's property, Grotius notes, public powers "have not only the right of defence but also the right to exact punishment."[7] The language of vindication and of punishment that was central to the earlier just war conception remains in Grotius's discussion, but the particular sort of injury that may be vindicated or punished has here been reduced to the violation of territory, whether actual or imminent. Whereas the older conception had conceived the ruler as a judge in determining whether a particular injustice that could justify the use of armed force existed, and if so, what would be necessary to restore justice and punish the perpetrator, on this new conception there is no need for any such exercise of judgment: If the border of a political community has been violated, that is plain for all to see, and as Grotius presents the case for preemptive resort to force, he also describes the imminence of the violation in terms of absolute certainty of the other's intention: "It is . . . required, that the danger be present and ready instantly to fall upon us."[8] The moral element of the decision to resort to armed force, which on the traditional conception worked through the judicial judgment of the ruler, disappears here: The right to use armed force is conferred automatically by the offender's action. All that remains within the sphere of judgment is to ensure that the reaction is proportionate to the fault. Sovereignty here is no longer a moral category.

Grotius also reshapes the conception of the law of nations, reformulating it in a way that could later be reshaped into a concept of international law. Throughout *De iure belli ac pacis* Grotius employs a layered understanding of various kinds of law and their proper interrelations. At the very beginning of the work, in section 1 of the preface, he anticipates his purpose to provide something new: "Few have treated of that law that exists between peoples, or between the rulers of peoples, whether based on nature, or established by divine decree, or grown out of custom and tacit agreements; and no one as yet has discussed it in a comprehensive and systematic way, important as it is to mankind that this be done."[9] In Book I he lays out his initial categorization: There are two fundamental kinds of law, natural law and voluntary law. Natural law (defined in Chapter I.10) is based on reason and "cannot be changed even by God himself." It includes not only "things that exist independent of the human will, but . . . many things which are a result of the exercise of that will." He explicitly mentions private property as exemplifying such a natural law.

Voluntary law (Chapter I.14ff.) includes both human laws and divine law. "Human law," Grotius writes, "is either civil law, or else a law more or less broad in scope than civil law. Civil law is that which issues from the civil power. . . . The law that is broader in scope is the law of nations, which derives its forceful authority from the will of all, or at least many, nations."[10] Grotius also distinguishes voluntary divine law, which issues in revelation and is not recognized by everyone, from the natural law, which, though based on divine will, is manifest for all in nature.[11] He notes that this law was given in two ways: to the entire human race (at creation, after the Flood, and in Christ) and to a specific people (the Hebrews through the law of Moses).

The older tradition of categorization had been somewhat different: divine or eternal law (*lex divinis*, *lex aeternae*), natural law (*lex naturale* or *ius naturale*), and the law of specific peoples or nations (*ius gentium*). Catholic doctrine tracing to Aquinas held that the law revealed in the Bible specifically published some elements of natural law and added new requirements. Nothing in natural law, on this conception, could be different from what is revealed, since God is the author of both. Indeed, one can know natural law in two ways, through reason or through revealed truth. Grotius shifts the grounds of the discussion. God's action lies behind the law of nature, but that simply means that the *lex aeternae* is reflected in the law of nature, and nothing that God has subsequently published in his voluntary law, found in the Bible, differs from this. Yet it is a separate kind of law, given in the two ways noted. This subtle redefinition on Grotius's part allows him in later discussions throughout *De iure belli ac pacis* to reframe law using Christian understandings as a form of human voluntary law, as when, in a typical way, he discusses the limits to be observed in fighting a just war in Book III: Some (very minimal) limits are imposed by the natural law; others (more restrictive) can be identified in the practices of classic Greece and Rome; and still others (the most restrictive) trace to the Christian law of charity. Christian law, earlier described as one form of the voluntary law of God, thus becomes transformed into the *ius gentium* common to Christian nations and the base for the law of nations formed among them by the "will of all, or at least many, nations." That the law of charity, Christian law, has this character is underscored by Grotius's comment that in the matter of enslavement of captives taken in war "the Mohammedans follow among themselves the practice of the Christians."[12] Moral requirements defined by religion, over and above requirements imposed by natural law, are thus a matter of particular versions of *ius gentium*.

For the Romans *ius gentium* was a plural category. Each of the peoples within Rome's domain had its own. All such laws had to be in accord with the *ius naturale*, of course, and they also had to be in accord with Roman law. A general "law of nations" founded on common consent was not part of the picture. One begins to see a shift in this understanding of the meaning of *ius gentium*, as noted in chapter 1 above, in the recovery and use of Roman concepts of law in the twelfth and thirteenth centuries, as the idea of a *ius gentium* common to European Christian societies developed. It is this latter idea, and not the Roman usage, on which Grotius builds. For him, when he speaks normatively and not descriptively, *ius gentium* refers to the international law founded on the "will of all, or at least many, nations," not to the particular laws of specific political communities and the people within them. These particular laws he identifies by a different term: civil law, *ius civile*.

In short, what we see here is the beginning of the modern notion of international law. It is founded on the agreement of nations, by their choice ("will") to agree. The law of nations may reflect the will of all nations, but it may not; the law of "many" may define what is the law of nations. And, in the context that Grotius was addressing, such law referred specifically to the nations of Europe. There might, in principle, be other laws of nations (such as in Islamic societies), or there might not. But Grotius was convinced that there was such a law of nations in Europe (which he refers to as "the Christian world"): "I am convinced . . . that there is a common law between nations which is valid for and in war."[13] He was also convinced that there were uncivilized portions of the world, which he terms "savage and inhuman," which do not even recognize the requirements of the law of nature.[14] Vitoria had earlier argued that the Indians of the New World could justly be punished by force of Spanish arms for acting in ways contrary to the law of nature.[15] Later generations of Europeans would similarly argue for the extension of the European law of nations over the world at large as implied by the goal of civilization. Indeed, the prominent author on international law Georg Schwarzenberger, in a work published as recently as 1967, could describe the law of war as founded on two standards: "the standard of civilization and the necessities of war."[16] On such thinking, "uncivilized" societies could and should be brought to understand the requirements regarding war and other relations among nations. But there is also the matter of otherwise civilized societies that are not among the "many" who, on Grotius's conception, can define the law of nations: For him the law is implicitly binding on them too, even though they have not explicitly joined their wills to its making.

In addition to this change in the understanding of natural law and the law of nations, Grotius redefines the inherited just war tradition as a body of laws that are externally binding and can, at least in principle, be externally enforced. The tradition he inherited, by contrast, was defined in moral terms: The principal element in the requirements for the resort to just war, for Aquinas and his successors, was the moral responsibility of the person in supreme political authority to care for the common good; the idea of just cause was defined in terms of reestablishing justice; the intention of a just war was defined in terms of the avoidance of wrong motives and the aim of establishing an orderly, just peace. This centrally moral conception still was robust in Luther, as seen in his thinking about the German peasants' rebellion. But Grotius's work was titled *Of the Laws of War and Peace*, not *Of the Morality of War and Peace*. Thus when he turns specifically to the requirements for undertaking war, in Book III, Chapter III, his title is "War That Is Legal or Formal according to the Law of Nations"; he does not speak here of "just war" but of "legal war"; and his principal requirement is that war be publicly declared, so that all its features may be known and judged by all. This is quite a significant change. In the context of the Westphalian system of international order, it effectively removes moral considerations from the table.

Where conduct in war is concerned we see a similar shift to the (externally binding) rules to be observed; yet in this case, the shift in thinking had begun earlier, with the codification of statements of military discipline for the armies of common men that became the norm for the modern period. Here the older frame was the virtue morality of chivalry, into which a knight was socialized by intensive training and experience, so that he was expected to conduct himself, in war and out, according to an internalized sense of right and wrong. This was, indeed, called *ius in bello*, *loi d'armes*, "law of war," but the law in question was an internal one, the "law of one's members," operating much like the internal sense of right and wrong understood as given by natural law. With the rise of armies of common men, who had not experienced such socialization, codes of military discipline began to appear, codes that boiled down the fundamental requirements of the older internalized sense of what is right to do in war and changed them to rules that were to be externally enforced on the common soldiers, immediately by their military superiors and ultimately by their sovereign. It is this latter view that Grotius adopts. Subsequently the "law of war" is a body of rules laying out right and wrong behavior, whose immediate effect depends on the promulgation and enforcement of these rules in particular political communities and whose content depends ultimately on international agreement.

Grotius's rethinking of just war, natural law, and the law of nations thus puts a great many new ideas on the table. Broadly, they became incorporated into the international system that coalesced in Europe after the Peace of Westphalia. But in important respects they pose problems. First, these new ideas are often at odds in significant ways with the deeper traditions, especially those of natural law and just war. Second, they open the way to imperialism, as the notion of civilization agreed to by those nations whose common will establishes the law of nations is in principle binding on other nations and can be imposed on them. And third, under the umbrella of consensus there remain many points of contention. One of these is the real-world meaning of the idea that the defense of national territory and the people inhabiting it represents the primary, or perhaps the only, justification for war. In its original historical context, set by the religiously motivated wars of the sixteenth century and early seventeenth, this provided a way of avoiding wars justified by the appeal to "true" religion and aimed at punishing and suppressing "false" religion; thus the new conception offered the hope of minimizing the resort to war. But the frequent "sovereigns' wars" of the next century vigorously tested the limits of this idea. Another point of contention would arise later: the degree to which the law of nations, founded on national consent, can be regarded as actually binding and not simply a statement of agreement to be bound if desired or a *lex ferenda* that nations should seek to follow but cannot be required to follow, especially if they have not formally consented to be bound by the law. A third contended issue in the meaning of the law of nations would not arise until the emergence of positive international law: the relation of this law to customary law, the actual behavior of states based on their own understandings of what is right. I will not examine all these issues comprehensively, but they all have to do with how the idea of sovereignty and its relation to the use of armed force have developed in the centuries between Grotius and our own time.

The Peace of Westphalia Itself

The Peace of Westphalia (1648), which ended the Thirty Years' War, incorporated the same fundamental ideas and shifts in conception that Grotius had intellectually systematized. But it would be going too far to suggest that the members of the delegations at the conferences that shaped the series of treaties known collectively as the Peace of Westphalia were consciously working from Grotius's formulation. Rather, as is the case with Grotius's work itself, it is better to see what they did as reflecting the consensus that had been growing during the previous century and more about the nature of political communities, sovereignty, and the magnified place for defense as conferring justification for the resort to armed force. The Thirty Years' War, which raged over most of northern Europe from 1618 to 1648, can be seen as the last of the post-Reformation wars of religion. More accurately, though, it was a war over religion only during its first part, when what was at issue in the German states was whether to roll back the concluding principle of the first of the religious wars, which had taken place within the empire, that each of the rulers of the states included in the empire could determine which would be the established religion in that state. This principle, known by its Latin formulation as the principle of *cuius regio, eius religio*, had resulted in the erosion of the Catholic population and Catholic power in the empire, and the start of the Thirty Years' War can be traced to the desire of the emperor and his Catholic allies to reverse this state of affairs. In the Netherlands the Thirty Years' War was but a new name and a new phase in the Dutch war for independence (which has been called the Eighty Years' War), with the Protestant Dutch ranged against Catholic Spain, which in 1618 retained its overlordship of what is now Belgium and wanted to recover overlordship over the rest of the Low Countries. All the countries of these two regions were drawn into the fight, and Sweden, an independent power and also strongly Protestant, came in on the Protestant side in the German arena of the conflict. Holy war rhetoric magnified and swirled on both sides, and the conduct of the war was notoriously bloody and unrestrained.

The prospect of being encircled on the north by a combined Spanish-Imperial alliance linking two branches of the House of Habsburg brought France into the struggle about midway, in 1635, and the character of the conflict gradually changed from a religious war to a dynastic struggle for position and power on the continent. A strategic stalemate ensued, and this, coupled with the devastation and exhaustion of the northern European region, led to the effort to achieve a negotiated end to the conflict. That end was the series of treaties signed between May and October of 1648, known collectively as the Peace of Westphalia. There were three treaties: the Peace of Münster between the Dutch Republic and the Kingdom of Spain, signed in January 1648 and ratified in May of that year; and two treaties both signed on October 24, 1648, the Treaty of Münster between the Holy Roman Emperor and France and their respective allies, and the Treaty of Onasbrück among the emperor, the empire, and Sweden and their respective allies.

While the bulk of the content of the treaties composing the Peace of Westphalia had to do with particular territorial settlements and related matters, the Peace also established three larger points: the recognition by all parties of the principle of *cuius regio, eius religio*, reached in the Peace of Augsburg of 1555; the right of free practice of religion to Christians living in states where their faith was not the established, officially recognized one; and—most importantly for the question on which this book focuses—recognition of each party's sovereignty over its lands, its population, and its agents abroad by all parties to the settlement.

While these three provisions represented major steps in the context of the mid-seventeenth century, after more than a century of warfare over religion, their radical nature is difficult to appreciate from the perspective of the present day, when the Westphalian conception of sovereignty provides the base for the international order and is written into the Charter of the United Nations; when freedom of religion, though not universal, is a widely recognized ideal and an element of international human rights law; and when religious establishment, where it has not entirely faded away, means a great deal less than it did in 1648. Their interrelation and whether all were genuinely necessary to achieve the end of warfare over religion may also be questioned from the perspective of the present day.

One issue has to do with the interrelation between religious establishment and the freedom to practice faiths not established: These are inherently in tension with each other. Religious establishment, by its nature, involves the temporal government in the matter of religious belief and practice, while the protection of freedom of religion makes such belief and practice ultimately a matter of individual preference and choice. Though on the Gelasian principle the spheres of religion and temporal government were separate, in practice all through the Middle Ages and into the modern period exactly what this meant was repeatedly tested, and there was a broad consensus that among the responsibilities of sovereigns was to protect the normative Christian religion. This meant, in practice, the periodic use of temporal power against dissident and heretic Christian groups and against Jews and Muslims living in lands where Catholic Christianity was the norm. In the era of the Reformation, this history and the assumptions associated with it provided the rationale for both Catholics and Protestants to argue for the use of force by the temporal authorities to enforce their own version of Christianity and to suppress the other. The results included forced conversions, what in the late twentieth century came to be called "ethnic cleansing," governmentally sanctioned mass killings like the St. Bartholomew's Day Massacre in France, and warfare between political communities over which religion would be the one officially sanctioned. The assumptions underlying this commonality of religious belief and practice were understood to provide a necessary focus for the unity of the society; the idea that there could be a single unified society in which more than one form of religion was accepted and practiced was strange indeed. In this context the settlement of *cuius regio, eius religio* reached in the Peace of Augsburg and renewed in the Peace of Westphalia was a major step for Europe as a whole, but no step at all for individual temporal societies with their own sovereigns.

Yet in 1648, the fact was that many such societies were religiously divided, and so long as the power of the temporal authorities was used to try to enforce a single form of belief and practice, conflict was inevitable. Toleration of religious difference was a radical move in the context of religious establishment and all that undergirded it, but such toleration offered a way out of continuing conflict over religion, though it was inherently in tension with the idea and practice of religious establishment by the governing authorities. The long run since then has preferred religious freedom to establishment, but there remain strong forces in support of religious uniformity in parts of the world, and the tension between these two approaches to the relation between temporal governing authority and freedom of religious belief and practice is far from resolved.

The central concern of this book, though, is with the redefinition of sovereignty set in place by the Peace of Westphalia. Again, in its immediate context this provided a way of settling conflict rooted in religious difference, and it connected directly to the principle of *cuius regio, eius religio*: If each independent political community had sovereignty over its own territory, people, and laws, then no outside claimant had the right to seek to change the existing state of affairs in any such community. The emphasis on territorial integrity and national self-determination here aimed at establishing them as having absolute priority over claims of outsiders based on appeals to transcendent (that is, religious) conceptions of truth. But so long as an outside power could claim to be acting on behalf of an oppressed religious minority, all of the earlier thinking on the right of resistance to tyranny provided a justification for intervention by such a power. Thus the Peace of Westphalia's provision for toleration of religious difference was also essential, because it aimed to take away such possible justifications for the use of military force by taking away the ostensible cause, oppression due to religious difference. All three of these major provisions in the Peace of Westphalia—*cuius regio, eius religio*, toleration of religious difference, and territorial independence—tied together as an interconnected whole.

The Peace of Westphalia's provision regarding each party's sovereignty over its territory and populace did not, by itself, shift the understanding of sovereignty from being focused on the ruler to being focused on the territory, people, and laws of each particular political community; that shift depended on the Westphalian settlement's being read through the intellectual lens provided by Grotius and the thinkers of the century before him whose rethinking of the matter of sovereignty he built on and systematized. Read in itself, the language of the Peace of Westphalia was compatible with the older conception of sovereignty as centered on the ruler without temporal superior. The formulation *cuius regio, eius religio*, indeed, on the face of it seems to assume such an understanding of sovereignty, and in its original context, the Peace of Augsburg in 1555, that older conception of sovereignty still obtained. Negotiated treaties ending conflicts, like those of both the Peace of Augsburg and the Peace of Westphalia, rightly focus on stating mutually agreed-upon remedies for the causes of the conflict; they are inherently conservative and do not aim at creating conceptual change in the relations between the parties, for the success of such treaties depends on those very relationships. But after the conflict is ended, the provisions of such treaties are read in a different context, and they may take on new meanings. That is what happened with regard to the conception of sovereignty, as later thinkers read the new emphasis on territorial integrity and independence provided for by the Peace of Westphalia through the intellectual developments of the century before it, and particularly through the thinking of Grotius.

Post-Westphalian Thinking on Sovereignty: Pufendorf and Vattel

This section considers two major thinkers who contributed to this rethinking and redefinition of the meaning of the treatment of sovereignty after the Westphalian settlement: Samuel Freiherr von Pufendorf (1632–94) and Emerich de Vattel (1714–67). Both wrote influentially on the concept of the law of nations and international order; both approached this from a perspective essentially Grotian, conceiving the sovereignty of political communities as following from the natural right that the members of that community have to defend themselves and their property. On this conception both the exercise of sovereign authority and the fundamental right to use armed force follow from this source. A variety of other writers from the period between them might well also be considered in connection with these ideas, but Pufendorf and Vattel stand as a pair of bookends to the development: Pufendorf at the beginning, Vattel when it has been effectively accomplished. For the sake of economy, then, I will limit this discussion to these two.

Pufendorf's major work dealing with this subject—or group of subjects—is *The Law of Nature and Nations* (*De jure naturae et gentium*), published in 1672, cited here from the fifth English edition of 1749. A shorter work based on it, *On the Duty of Man and Citizen* (*De officio hominis et civis*) first appeared in 1675. These works are heavily influenced by Grotius, though they also reflect close engagement with Hobbes. Indeed, Pufendorf's conception of how the state is formed follows the outline of Hobbes's thinking, though Pufendorf is sharply critical of Hobbes's idea of the social contract as producing an all-powerful Leviathan. For Pufendorf what creates the state is not only the need for defense but human "sociability," and the individual and collective agreements that bring the state into being are described as covenants of mutual responsibility between the individual members of the political community and the community that results. "Men only are a sufficient Defence against the Wickedness of Men," Pufendorf writes, and "to this End it is necessary that many should join together."[17] They do so by individually and collectively joining in covenants for their mutual good; Pufendorf describes this as analogous to the covenant of marriage and the resulting unifying bond of marriage.[18] He goes on:

> By the Means of these Covenants then a Multitude of men are so united and incorporated, as to form a civil State, which is conceived to exist like *one Person*, endued with Understanding and Will. . . . So that the most proper Definition of a civil State seems to be this: "It is a compound moral Person, whose Will, united and tied together by those Covenants which before passed among the Multitude, is deemed the Will of all, to the End, that it may use and apply the Strength and Riches of private persons towards maintaining the common Peace and Security."[19]

The state in exercising its will, he goes on, "makes use of either a single Person, or of a Council, according as the supreme Command has been conferred."[20] The result is either a monarchy or some form of collective governance. Pufendorf uses the word "sovereignty" for the exercise of the will of the whole, but it is clear nonetheless that this is a delegated concept from the society as a whole. "Sovereignty appears to be established . . . in a lawful manner, upon the voluntary Consent and Submission of the respective Members. This then is the nearest and immediate Cause, from which sovereign Authority, as a moral Quality, doth result."[21] Or as he puts the relationship a bit later, "A State is a Moral Body conceived to act by one Will," and "that one Will, which we attribute to the State, must be produced by the agreement of all Persons, to submit their own private Wills to the Will of one Man, or one Assembly of Men, on whom the Government has been conferred."[22]

When Pufendorf wrote, the Westphalian settlement was a quarter-century old, and while it had generally held, Germany had not yet recovered from the devastation of the Thirty Years' War, and the relative rights and priorities of the emperor and the rulers of the various states within the empire continued to be a matter of contention. In 1667 he had written a pseudonymous pamphlet criticizing the governance of the House of Austria over Germany; this presaged his strong emphasis, in the works of 1672 and 1675, on the moral character of the state defined as the sum of the individual moral wills of its people.

I have stressed the moral character of the idea of sovereignty as conceived normatively in the idea of just war as it first came together in the twelfth and thirteenth centuries. There the exercise of sovereignty proceeded from the sovereign authority's responsibility for the common good of the political community, defined by natural law and consisting in the protection of order, justice, and peace. When Pufendorf speaks of the state as a "moral body," though, he is thinking of it as founded on the moral obligation for self-preservation of each of its members, and the fundamental moral obligation of the state is thus its own self-preservation, that is, its defense against attacks and threats. When he speaks of the moral responsibility of the sovereign authority, what he means is the responsibility to fulfill the terms of the covenant between the person or persons who exercise such authority and those who have, by their covenant, delegated such authority to them. The language is similar, but the conceptions are quite different. Thus when Pufendorf describes the justification for the resort to armed force, it is not in terms of the vindication of justice (as in the older tradition) but in terms of self-preservation: "The just causes of engaging in war come down to the preservation and protection of our lives and property against unjust attack, or the collection of what is due to others but has been denied, or the procurement of reparations for wrong inflicted and of assurance for the future."[23] What is allowed to the individual is allowed to the state. The individual is sovereign in his own right in the natural state, and in covenanting to create the political community he delegates that right to whomever exercises authority on behalf of the community as a whole. As in Grotius, then, sovereign authority and the right to use armed force derive from the individual's right of self-defense; in the political community, that sovereign authority is delegated to others, and the state has no right to employ armed force except in self-defense. The vindication of justice is thus reduced to defense against attack.

For Vattel, only each individual state can determine the justice of its actions, and this follows from the fundamental nature of the state as having come together for the common welfare of its people and therefore having the right and obligation to preserve itself and its members. He summarizes the "general principles" by defining states and the relations among them in the law of nations in these terms:

> (1) Nations or States are political bodies, societies of men who have united together and combined their forces, in order to procure their mutual welfare and security.

> (2) Such a society has its own affairs and interests; . . . it . . . becomes a moral person having an understanding and a will peculiar to itself, and susceptible at once of obligations and of rights. . . .
>
> (18) Since men are by nature equal, and their individual rights and obligations the same, as coming equally from nature, Nations, which are composed of men and may be regarded as so many free persons living together in a state of nature, are by nature equal and hold from nature the same obligations and the same rights. . . .
>
> (19) From this equality it necessarily follows that what is permitted or prohibited to one Nation is equally permitted or prohibited to every other Nation. . . .
>
> (20) The intrinsic justice of their conduct is another matter which it is not for others to make a definitive judgment upon; so that what one may do another may do, and they must be regarded in the society of mankind as having equal rights.[24]

This formulation effectively removes the idea of an overarching justice binding all political communities to certain behavior from the table. Each nation has its own right to make its own decisions as to its behavior, internally and externally, as to what may serve its "mutual welfare and security." Only if this threatens other states may they, by the same right, resist. If there is no external threat, then states should be left to make their own decisions. The earlier idea that sovereigns have a moral obligation to secure justice even in other political communities when justice is violated (the fundamental justification of resistance to tyranny) is entirely removed from consideration here. Vattel's concern was to establish the equality of all states in their relations with one another, and to do this he reserved all internal matters to each state itself, free from outside interference. This formulation cast a long shadow, both positively and negatively. While each state has a "duty to itself" that includes both its self-preservation as a state and the preservation of "the lives of its members,"[25] this is not a duty for other states, and they have no right to interfere in how a particular state acts regarding these duties. Indeed, as Vattel develops his argument, it is clear that the duty and right of self-preservation (that is, the duty and right of self-defense against other states) are paramount: "The right of self-preservation carries with it the right to do whatever is necessary for that purpose."[26]

The only mitigation of the laissez-faire character of this conception of the relations between states is in Vattel's argument that there is a natural duty to assist others in reaching their own perfection. But as he states the implications of this duty, it is entirely for the purpose of denying one nation the right to seek to damage another: "This general principle prohibits all nations from evil practices tending to create disturbance in another state, to foment discord, to corrupt its citizens, to alienate its allies, to sully its reputation, and to deprive it of its natural advantages."[27] Vattel's description of international society in terms of juridically equal states, each of which makes its own decisions as to how to secure its basic purposes, and each of which has no right to interfere with the decisions of another, thus gives the right of defense a new prominence. Only when one state's actions threaten another does the latter have the right to use armed force as a result of the duty to defend itself. But if a state or a group of states seeks to force another to act differently in internal matters, then the latter has the right to push back, defending itself against such interference.

As to the matter of sovereignty, for Vattel ruling authority derives explicitly from beneath. The right to make war follows from the duty and right of self-preservation in every individual, and in the state this right and this duty are transferred to the state and vested in its ruling authority. Those who hold this authority thus have the right to make decisions for the entire state, for, once given, that right cannot be taken back.[28] The only rights possessed by the ruler are those delegated to the state by its individual members and vested in the ruler; yet once the ruler has these rights, they have no real checks on what they may decide.

Vattel is an especially important figure, in that his conception of the international order as composed of independent and juridically equal states, with each state having the right to make its own determination of what is just and no other state having the right to challenge this unless it poses a threat, is essentially the conception that solidified in the years after him. Convention calls this "the Westphalian system," but it might well be called "the Vattel system." In terms of the resort to force, Vattel's aim was to emphasize the right of defense and thus to prevent states from aggressing against one another. But in fact his stress on the right to do "whatever is necessary" for self-preservation, as determined by the ruling authority in each state, took the form of what came to be called the *liberum jus ad bellum*, the free right of each state to wage war on its own determination of what is necessary for its own self-preservation. Vattel's conception fit well within the historical frame of the "sovereigns' wars" of the eighteenth century. There was no longer any justification for, say, a Holy Roman emperor to make war to seek to impose the Catholic religion on a Protestant state within the empire; so his conception ruled out the start of wars like the Thirty Years' War. Similarly, it provided justification for the resistance to Napoleon undertaken by an alliance of states not many decades after he wrote. But it made the matter of determining whether to begin a war a matter for each state, on what would later be called its determination of its "interests." And it opened the door to what an earlier age had called tyrannical rule within states by making the quality of rule not the business of any other state. With Vattel we are firmly in the age of the modern international system.

Notes

1. Reichberg, Syse, and Begby, eds., *Ethics of War*, 385–86.
2. Quoted in ibid., 310–12.
3. Ibid., 379–83.
4. Ibid., 150–51.
5. *Summa theologiae* II/II, Q. 40, A. 1.
6. Vanderpol, *La Doctrine scolastique du droit de guerre*, 250.
7. Book II, Chapter XVI; Reichberg, Syse, and Begby, *Ethics of War*, 404.
8. Book II, Chap. I.5; Grotius, *Law of War and Peace*, 73.
9. Grotius, *Law of War and Peace*, 3.
10. Chapter I.14; Grotius, *Law of War and Peace*, 23.
11. Book I, Chapter I.15; Grotius, *Law of War and Peace*, 23.
12. Book III, Chapter VII.9; Grotius, *Law of War and Peace*, 329.
13. Preface, Section 28; Grotius, *Law of War and Peace*, 10.
14. Book I, Chapter I.12; Grotius, *Law of War and Peace*, 22.
15. *De indis*, Q. 3, A. 1; Reichberg, Syse, and Begby, *Ethics of War*, 300.
16. Schwarzenberger, *The Frontiers of International Law*, 197.
17. *The Law of Nature and Nations*, Book VII, Chapter II; von Pufendorf, *The Law of Nature and Nations*, 5th ed., 631.
18. Section XII; Pufendorf, *Law of Nature and Nations*, 641.
19. Section XIII: Pufendorf, *Law of Nature and Nations*, 641.
20. Section XIV; Pufendorf, *Law of Nature and Nations*, 642.
21. Chapter III, Section I: Pufendorf, *Law of Nature and Nations*, 651.
22. Chapter IV, Section I; Pufendorf, *Law of Nature and Nations*, 657.

23. Pufendorf, *On the Duty of Man and Citizen*, Book II, Chapter 16.2; Reichberg, Syse, and Begby, *Ethics of War*, 457.
24. Vattel, *The Law of Nations; or Principles of the Law of Nature*, introduction; Reichberg, Syse, and Begby, *Ethics of War*, 506–7.
25. Vattel, *Law of Nations*, Book I, Chapter II, Section 17; Reichberg, Syse, and Begby, *Ethics of War*, 507.
26. Vattel, *Law of Nations*, Book I, Chapter II, Section 18; Reichberg, Syse, and Begby, *Ethics of War*, 507.
27. Vattel, *Law of Nations*, Book I, Section 20.
28. Vattel, *Law of Nations*, Book III, Chapter I, Section 4; Reichberg, Syse, and Begby, *Ethics of War*, 508.

5

Transitions in the Conception of Sovereignty

Reprise: Challenges to the Older Conception

Why did the older conception of sovereignty found in Western thought about politics and the use of force not endure? Daniel Philpott, in his *Revolutions in Sovereignty*, argues that two historical revolutions in ideas account for the rise of the modern conception of sovereignty: first, in a development that culminated in the Peace of Westphalia, the replacement of medieval Christendom by a system of independent states in Europe, brought into being as a result of the Protestant Reformation; second, and much later, the end to the colonial system around 1960 and the global spread of this state system.[1] Jean Bethke Elshtain, in *Sovereignty: God, State, and Self*, similarly identifies the idea of sovereignty with the rise of the state system, tracing this to revolutions in thought associated with the Reformation.[2] Other recent authors have described a somewhat more complicated process of transformation in forms of political order, without focusing on the idea of sovereignty itself. Francis Fukuyama in *The Origins of Political Order* follows the historical story only as far as the French Revolution but describes a more complex development to which different major world cultures have contributed distinctively, with the European state producing not a single model but four, of which the most successful was that of "accountable government," represented historically by England and Denmark, states that "were able to develop both strong rule of law and accountable government, while at the same time building strong centralized states capable of national mobilization and defense."[3] There is more than an echo of Vattel here, but more of Locke, and a background chorus is provided by the theorists from Vitoria to Grotius who first began to think of governmental authority as imposed not from the top downward but rather from the populace upward. But for the latter to be conceived and institutionalized as truly accountable, in the sense

Fukuyama has in mind, still remained to be achieved when these thinkers were done, though the concept of sovereignty itself had changed character decisively. If one looks in a different direction, to Niall Ferguson's sweeping account of the development of government and empires in *Civilization*, the guiding perspective is economic history, and the matter of how sovereignty is understood does not, for practical purposes, figure at all.[4] All these studies, as well as an earlier wave of scholarship focused on the ideal of the international order of states becoming something more and more like a world government, proceed out of different concerns and represent different perspectives.

My own view, developed in the previous chapters, is that the conception of sovereignty is of essential importance to how all sorts of matters having to do with political life and government are understood and what expectations are directed toward them. From this perspective Ferguson's study provides important nuance to the way history has actually developed, but there is a deeper story to that history which economic history does not seek to probe. Fukuyama importantly draws attention to the different ways major world cultures have conceived of life in a political community, its purposes, and its government, and while his study does not end up with the edginess of his mentor Samuel Huntington's concern about the likelihood of a future "clash of civilizations,"[5] these two thinkers provide a powerful reminder that the conceptualizations and institutionalizations of the West are not the only markers on the board of relations among nations and the possibilities of the use of armed force. I return to this matter in the next chapter.

Finally, in my judgment there are two problems with the ways Philpott and Elshtain handle the matter of the rise of the modern conception of sovereignty. First, they treat the category of sovereignty as a conception only identified with the modern state system. To be sure, the modern conception of sovereignty is tied up with the modern state system, but as the previous chapters show, there is a much deeper history of thought and political practice focused on the meaning of sovereignty as a category, and the emergence of the modern idea of sovereignty is not properly understood unless it is placed within the frame of this earlier history and set off against the conception of sovereignty found there. This leads to the second problem I find with how Philpott and Elshtain treat the matter of sovereignty. Identifying the modern idea of sovereignty as beginning with the Protestant Reformation, as they do, places the beginning of this idea somewhat too late. Rather, as I have shown, the conception of sovereignty already began to change before the Reformation began, and the Protestant thinkers who contributed to the refashioning of the idea of sovereignty were building on concerns and arguments already voiced before them. This is not to discount the importance of the Reformation, which advanced and modified the resulting new conceptions powerfully, and which in its opposition to the established Catholic order contributed decisively to the breakdown of the sense of commonality on which the earlier understanding of the basis of sovereignty depended. The Protestant thinkers examined in chapter 3 provide several important windows into this development. But in my view, the Reformation should not be regarded as beginning the conceptual change in thinking about political community and sovereignty that differentiates medieval and early modern political thought from the forms that succeeded them; rather, the cultural and political divide created by the Reformation completed trends that were already under way.

The story told in the previous chapters is one of rethinking the fundamental assumptions underlying the older conception of sovereignty as the moral responsibility of the ruler for the common good. Of these fundamental assumptions, arguably the most important was the idea of natural law, because all the other underlying assumptions were understood as expressions of the natural order that natural law described.

The conception of natural law that came together in the West beginning in the twelfth century and that endured until well into the modern period (longer in some contexts, not so long in others) rested on the Roman understanding of natural law and its relation to *ius gentium*, the Roman term for the laws (or more broadly, the controlling moral and legal conceptions, expressed as rules of behavior) of particular peoples (*gentes*) within the empire. But the conception that came together in the Middle Ages was not identical with the Roman one on which it built. There were two main differences. First, and especially after the intellectual synthesis between reason and revelation achieved by Thomas Aquinas, Western thought regarded natural law as able to be known not by reason alone, but also, at least in major respects, through revelation. Since, on the conceptions of Western thinkers, there could be no difference between natural law and divine law, insofar as revelation provided knowledge of divine law, this was also knowledge of natural law. The possibility that what was known by revelation and reason might be contradictory was thus ruled out. This provided an implicit challenge to what non-Christian peoples understood to be natural law, if that contradicted the (Western) Christian conception: The non-Christian peoples must not be using their reason rightly.

The second main difference between the Western Christian and the earlier Roman conceptions of natural law, *ius gentium*, and their interrelation had to do with the way the *ius gentium* was conceived. On the Roman understanding this concept was inherently plural in nature: The different peoples within the empire each had its own form of *ius gentium*, each worthy or not depending on the degree to which it reflected the *ius naturale*, natural law. Roman civil law (*ius civile*) was, on these terms, a form of *ius gentium*, though it held primacy over the others in that the positive law of Rome trumped the provisions of local laws in cases of conflict between them. But in the medieval Western context *ius gentium* came to refer to the "common law" of European Christian nations as a collective. Since this *ius gentium* was implicitly tutored by Christian revelation, what it provided represented a truth above and beyond simply the customs of Europeans as a "people," and for practical purposes it was sometimes difficult to distinguish from the natural law.

The implications of all this came to a head first in efforts to deal intellectually with the Spanish encounter with the Indians of the New World. Vitoria, generally sympathetic to the rights of the Indians as against what he regarded as exaggerated claims for Spanish dominion over them, held that "before arrival of the Spaniards these barbarians [the Indians] possessed true dominion, both in public and private affairs."[6] This followed, he argued, as a right from natural law. And the Indians could not be held to the standard of behavior laid out in Christian revelation, because they were not bound to accept this revelation as truth.[7] But, Vitoria argued, "the Spaniards have the right to travel and dwell in these countries, so long as they do no harm to the barbarians, and cannot be prevented by them from doing so," and the Spaniards might use force to secure this right. He referred his reasoning on this to the *ius gentium* as understood in Europe, "which either is or derives from natural law."[8] The possibility of taking seriously any opposition to this conclusion from the point of view of the Indians' own *ius gentium* was not considered. The European *ius gentium*, then, was understood to occupy a privileged place in setting the standards for the relations among the Spanish and the Indians. Vitoria's reasoning here was not the same as that which gave Roman civil law priority over the local laws of peoples in the empire; that was a matter of the primacy of Roman positive law over subject peoples. His argument was rather that the European *ius gentium* must be accepted by all nations as applying to them. This way of thinking prepared the way for the development of this concept into the idea of a common "law of nations" in the West in the thought of modern thinkers, as we have seen in the cases of Grotius, Pufendorf, and Vattel, and for extending its standards in the name of "civilization" to the rest of the world in the spread of colonialism.

But these last comments get ahead of our story. As far as it concerns the undermining of the conception of natural law on which the conception of sovereignty as moral responsibility for the common good is based, the European encounter with the Indians set in motion a fundamental empirical test of the genuine universal nature of this conception of natural law. The example of Vitoria shows how two ultimately contradictory responses to the encounter with the Indians were made: on the one hand, to assert the primacy of the European understanding of natural law and its implications; on the other hand, to assert that the Indians possessed innate rights that needed to be respected. In the context of the development of Spanish colonialism in the New World, this latter point was ignored and, for practical purposes, forgotten. But it fitted well with the developing currents in European thought that emphasized the rights of individuals and coherent groups as the basis for thinking about political life and government, and that led directly to the reformulation of the idea of sovereignty as rooted in those rights, or rather, specifically in the right of self-defense possessed by every individual and by coherent groups of people.

It is in this latter connection that the rise of Protestantism was important for the change in the conception of sovereignty. For here the medieval synthesis between what the Church understood and taught as revelation and natural law as understood by reason broke down, since the Protestants did not accept the authority of the Church over the content of revelation but rather shifted both the authority and the content of revelation to the Bible. The Protestant thinkers, moreover, emphasized this content over what might be known through natural law, so that the importance and scope of natural law were diminished.

This religious and intellectual shift took political form in the wars of religion between Catholics and Protestants that began early in the Reformation era and continued for fully a century. Here the claim was that the responsibility of the sovereign for the good of the political community extended to the maintenance of right religion, particularly its defense against heresy. This was a claim made on the basis of natural law, which was understood to include the responsibility of sovereigns for the defense of true religion. The (Catholic) German emperor first offered this reasoning in response to the spread of Protestantism in German states, but it was quickly adopted also by Protestant rulers seeking to maintain the establishment of the Protestant religion in their domains. But of course, what looked this way from the side of the governing authorities, whether Catholic or Protestant, looked very different from the side of those who were the object of coercive force, and they stressed their own rights in return. *Cuius regio, eius religio*, the formula that was the central feature of the Peace of Augsburg in 1555, which ended the initial Catholic-Protestant war in Germany, represented an attempt to hold on to the inherited idea of the extent of the responsibilities (and rights) of sovereign rulers, but the underlying resistance to such domination of religion by the governing authorities—again, whether these were Catholic or Protestant—continued, and the emphasis on individual and communal rights gradually became dominant. One effect of this shift was, as we have seen, the narrowing down of what could be claimed from natural law to a focus on the individual and communal right of self-defense and the resulting reformulation of the idea of rulership as derived by delegation from this individual and communal right. Another important result of the shift I have described was to strengthen the idea of individual states as bearers of responsibility for the defense of the rights of their communities. The changed understanding of sovereignty to a conception identified with each particular state resulted from the coincidence of these two distinguishable developments, both of which manifested the developing focus on individual and communal rights as what remained of the earlier idea of a universal natural law in the context of a fundamental cultural divide on values and authority.

Virtues and Faults in the Two Conceptions of Sovereignty

Understanding how a particular development in history has occurred and the reasons for it is not the same as saying that the development has been all to the good. The older conception of sovereignty framed in terms of the moral responsibility of temporal rulers with no temporal superiors to serve and protect the common good of the political communities they governed had several important virtues. First, it centered on the goods of political life as moral in nature, linking political order to justice and peace, both within each specific community and in the relations among communities. Second, it subordinated the use of power in the exercise of sovereignty to concern for the good of the community, thus tending to reinforce the bonds and commonalities of the political community and setting the exercise of genuine sovereignty directly against the self-serving character of tyranny. Third, in the context of the idea of just war it linked the right exercise of sovereignty explicitly to the maintenance of justice and the rectification of injustice. In this same context it imposed significant limits on the resort to the use of armed force by denying such use to anyone other than one in sovereign authority and for any purpose except in the exercise of sovereign responsibility for the common good. Fourth, despite the preference for monarchical government found in Aquinas and other thinkers of the period, it set parameters for good government that could apply to any particular form of government, not just monarchy alone. Fifth, it intentionally respected the rights of those governed, as well as persons in other political communities, since its purpose of serving justice and correcting injustice was set in the context of the judicial response to the claims of those governed whose rights had been violated. In cases of tyrannical oppression of members of another political community, the possibility of such a response was extended to assisting those whose rights had been violated in securing their claims for justice.

Of course, this conception of sovereignty also had faults. As those who formulated it recognized (and as we have seen specifically in the thought of Aquinas), the authority and power given to the ruler could be used for injustice: Tyranny was thus identified as the corruption of sovereignty, its self-service contrasting absolutely with the other-directed responsibilities of the true sovereign. Further, though it aimed intentionally at protecting and vindicating the rights of the members of the community governed, the thinkers who defined this conception of sovereignty as responsibility did not seek to provide any particular mechanism by which those people could influence the understanding or exercise of that responsibility. One could argue that such a mechanism was implicit in the idea of governing, as it is in the model of judicial decision making and action, since the existence of forms of injustice identified by the claims of members of the community reflecting violations of their individual rights would influence the sovereign to take steps to anticipate and prevent such particular forms of injustice in the future; that is, something like the effect of judicial precedent could be inferred to operate within this understanding of sovereignty and its exercise. But the theorists who shaped this conception of sovereignty never examined such a possibility, and indeed, the entire understanding of law from which they worked simply did not function that way. Though it was expected, on the model of the classical idea of virtue being built up through practice, that a sovereign could get better in the exercise of his responsibilities over time, this change was understood as a personal growth in moral capability, not as a political process involving the people governed in shaping their own government. And a third fault was revealed in the use of this idea of sovereignty as itself a justification for the denial of individual and communal rights in the religious wars of the Reformation era.

It was these faults that the new conception of sovereignty reached in the sixteenth and seventeenth centuries sought to correct. Unfortunately, the virtues of the old conception also suffered and were substantially or entirely lost in subsequent history. The state system that developed as the institutional form of the new conception of sovereignty aimed directly at preventing wars based on religion or other cultural or ideological differences, doing so by affirming the integrity of discrete political communities regardless of such differences among them. By focusing on defense against attack or the threat of attack from another state, this new system sought to prevent or at least limit the possibility of one such community attacking another. But this emphasis on the right of self-defense turned out to give individual rulers the liberty to claim the defense of the good of their particular state and its people as a reason for war against another state. This was the idea of the *liberum jus ad bellum* possessed by each individual state, which gave it the right to choose to make war in support of its interests. The frequent "sovereigns' wars" of the eighteenth century provide one kind of example of this, the Napoleonic wars of conquest another; and in actuality this conception of the sovereign right of individual states to make war at their own discretion, for their own interests, remained well into the twentieth century, when first the Kellogg-Briand Pact of 1928 and later the United Nations Charter of 1945 sought to remedy it by outlawing the resort to armed force by one state against another in the service of its own side in a dispute. This implicitly denied that the justice of any party's claim in a dispute could be sought by the resort to arms; rather, such resort was itself defined as the greatest injustice and rejected as a matter of principle. The use of armed force as such, except in self-defense against aggression, thus became identified as the problem with warfare, not the underlying causes that the earlier conception of sovereignty had understood as violations of justice needing to be remedied. The Kellogg-Briand pact did not succeed in ending the first resort to armed force, as the beginnings of World War II testify. Similar language, placed in the United Nations Charter, has done better, though new shapes of warfare have developed that circumvent this language. Importantly, though, by placing the onus on the first resort to force between states, this language effectively gave immunity to tyrannical uses of force within states, since the matter of justice in the right use of force was taken out of the picture.

The new conception of sovereignty, once embodied in the state system that came out of the Peace of Westphalia and cast as the legal framework of international order in the United Nations system, has thus provided the frame for the use of ruling authority and power for systematic assaults on the rights of some or all the people ruled. The international system has attempted to address this problem in various ways, most importantly through the growth of human rights law, through the Genocide Convention, and through the doctrine of "the responsibility to protect." It is to be noted that both the Genocide Convention and "the responsibility to protect" doctrine rest on a base provided by the growth of human rights law, intended to describe an international consensus by describing such rights and the need to protect them. Since the very understanding of sovereignty that eventually led to the abuses of individual and communal rights came out of an assertion of such rights, there is a certain irony here; perhaps a renewed assertion of the idea of such rights is not adequate to address the problem.

People and Their Rulers: Absolutism, Human Rights, and Community

The new conception of sovereignty reached early in the modern period was framed principally in terms of the natural right to self-protection possessed by individuals and communities of people. This responded, in general terms, to the breakdown of a broad conception of natural law that, under the circumstances of the discovery of new civilizations abroad and the emergence of new forms of Christianity in Europe, was used to provide the justification for what, from the perspective of dissenters, was effectively tyrannic usurpation of the rights of individuals and their communities. Tyranny, of course, was an older concept, and as we have seen, the framing of the older idea of sovereignty as responsibility for the common good set tyranny, defined as a ruler's pursuit of personal good over the common good, in opposition to genuine sovereignty. But in the early modern context the problem was somewhat different: the pursuit of the good of a part of the larger political community while opposing the good of another part. The older system did not include intellectual or political tools that were able to deal with this, and it tended to default to favoring the decisions and actions of the ruling authority or authorities over the people governed.

In the discussions in the previous chapters we have seen two examples of this. Aquinas, while severely criticizing tyrannical rule as such, counseled accepting it unless it is "excessive," and even in "intolerable" cases he argued that the tyrant should be removed not by the people but by other persons bearing ruling authority. Similarly, Luther, though agreeing with the German peasants that their economic welfare was being ignored, sided strongly with the authorities in putting the peasants down when they rebelled to seek relief. Likewise, while he supported the right of the Protestant German princes to reject the authority of the Catholic emperor and fight against him, he stridently opposed popular Protestant movements that sought relief by seceding and forming their own communities. The older tradition of sovereignty, though emphasizing the obligation of government to serve the common good by creating and maintaining a just and peaceful order, was thus interpreted so as to favor the imposition of order, even when that order maintained injustice. The new understanding of sovereignty, defining the responsibilities of government as a delegation upward of the natural right of the people and the community to self-protection, implicitly offered a correction to this imbalance in favor of order in the interpretation of the older tradition. Indeed, since the medieval theorists (including Aquinas) had stressed the importance of the right to rule's needing to be accepted by those ruled, it is even possible to regard the idea of the right of rule as delegated upward from the community as an expression of this older idea, not a newly forged one.

Unfortunately, and as a negative result of the positive ends intended, this new way of thinking redefined the right to use armed force so that it reduced the good to be served to the self-defense of the state's territory against attack from another state. What Grotius called "the ancient rights and privileges" of the inhabitants of a particular territory were respected only to the point of privileging the defense of such territory against efforts to impose outside domination. So long as a ruler acted to provide such defense, there was no reason contained in the new understanding of sovereignty that might call into question the nature of the rule in more general terms. To put this more directly, a ruler might govern with a heavy, even tyrannical, hand, but the new conception of sovereignty did not address this, and the new system of states accepted the possibility of such misrule so long as the territorial integrity of the state in question was maintained.

The historical shift in the conception of sovereignty thus came with a set of its own problems. Exemplifying the working of the law of unintended consequences, the institutionalization of the new conception of sovereignty in the Westphalian state system opened the door to the development of absolutist states and to an increased frequency of wars, all in the name of protection of the territorial integrity of the states in question. A further irony is that, even though the new idea of sovereignty and its institutionalization in the state system sought to avoid the justification of the use of armed force in the name of religion, it did not prevent the justification of such force in the service of nonreligious ideologies such as that of the French Revolution, fascism and communism in the twentieth century, and, at the end of the twentieth century and into the present, the resurgence of religious justification for war (though not warfare between states) in the form of the radical Islamist conception of jihad of the sword. Against all this, one might put the success of the growth of liberal democratic states, which developed on their own terms a conception of the importance of justice in domestic and international affairs, and perhaps even of the international system centered on the United Nations (though to some extent these are in tension). The new conception of sovereignty and its institutionalization in the state system have thus provided the base for both positive and negative developments in the relations between peoples and their rulers and between political communities. Though liberal democratic states and absolutist ones share this common base, they differ critically in that the values and institutional structures of liberal democracies have emphasized the central element in the older conception of sovereignty: the responsibility of government to serve the broader common good of the society as a whole. In the liberal democracies the rationale for this builds on respect for the rights of the people in general, while the idea of responsibility for the common good in the older conception of sovereignty expressed the obligation to follow the goods of politics as defined in natural law.

Yet there may be less to this difference than the fact of the difference suggests. Paul Ramsey, examining the necessary foundations for community to exist among people, criticizes the early Utilitarians for failing to consider the value basis on which their arguments for utility depend.[9] For Ramsey, their arguments made sense only when the existing social cohesion of their society and the personal and social values making for this cohesion were taken into account; the Utilitarians' reasoning by itself could not produce such cohesion. Ramsey, a Christian theologian, argues for Christian love as necessary for the formation of human community, but his reasoning in fact bears broader implications for the necessity of common personal and social values in a society for a genuine community to exist there.

Modern liberal democratic states, in contrast to those in which absolutism in various forms has triumphed, have managed to hold on to the core values of the older conception of sovereignty as responsibility for the common good: that good rule means concern for others, namely, the people governed, rather than oneself; that this is expressed in the maintenance of an order that serves justice and peace within the society governed and in relations with other societies; that while the resort to armed force may be necessary to combat and rectify injustice, it must be limited to the proper purposes of government; and that all this needs to be understood with reference to the personal rights of the membership of the society as a whole. For liberal democratic societies, the modern emphasis on human rights has served to focus all these values, and accordingly these societies have taken the lead in seeking to place respect for human rights in the forefront in defining the international order. This emphasis is certainly congruent with the shift in thinking about sovereignty that took place early in the modern period. But the liberal democratic understanding of human rights cannot be assumed to be universal across the globe. The history of the development of international human rights law shows an important lack of consensus on the nature and sources of the rights recognized. The efforts of the United Nations to monitor and enforce international human rights law have at best been mixed. In particular contexts a degree of consensus has formed around the idea that egregious violations of basic human rights should not be tolerated, and though the coalescence of the doctrine of the responsibility to protect seeks to establish respect for such basic rights as a domestic and international norm, in practice what this means for particular cases and how to enforce it have varied greatly. How, then, to conceive of a moral basis for human community that would counter the trends toward tyrannical absolutism that have historically emerged out of the modern conception of sovereignty and its institutionalization in the state system?

Returning now to the matter of internal dissatisfaction with a ruler within a state, the state system itself has tended to impose a preference for the existing order as against not only external aggression but also internal rebellion and revolution. Three reasons for this can be identified. First, the ruling parties of tyrannically governed states typically have both friends and foes in the international order, with each side behaving as might be expected with regard to the replacement of the regime in question, favoring or opposing efforts to replace them. Second, the bias against the use of armed force across state borders tends to give an advantage to the military and police establishments of the government in question against its opponents. And third, the outcomes of regime change, even when the regime in question is atrociously bad, can never be completely foreseen, and inevitably they produce their own evils. These are pragmatic reasons, though. The older conception of sovereignty tended toward a preference for existing forms of order because on its terms order was understood as necessary for justice and peace, and proponents of this conception never really faced the practicalities of how to ensure that the ideal of a just and peaceful order, the achievement of the goods of political life that serve the common good of the political community, should be sought when the ruling authority embodying order uses that authority for ends other than justice and peace. The older conception of sovereignty was replaced for good, if historically occasioned, reasons. Whether its virtues can be recovered and generally institutionalized apart from its vices is the central problem. Yet it would be good to seek to do so. The ideal that the older conception expressed remains, and it is more general in its nature and universal in its scope than what is provided for in the conception of sovereignty that has replaced it. The older conception systematically rejected the misuse of order in the form of various sorts of tyranny, though it hedged on how to deal with it in the realm of practical life; the modern conception of sovereignty actually holds open the possibility of tyrannical rule so long as the ruler maintains the integrity of the political community's borders. This is a critical difference.

Notes

1. Philpott, *Revolutions in Sovereignty.*
2. Elshtain, *Sovereignty: God, State, and Self.*
3. Fukuyama, *The Origins of Political Order*, 334.
4. Ferguson, *Civilization: The West and the Rest.*
5. Huntington, "The Clash of Civilizations?," 22.
6. *De indis* Q. 1, Conclusion; Reichberg, Syse, and Begby, *Ethics of War*, 293.
7. *De indis* Q. 2; Reichberg, Syse, and Begby, *Ethics of War*, 294–99.
8. *De indis* Q. 3, A. 1; Reichberg, Syse, and Begby, *Ethics of War*, 300.
9. Ramsey, *Basic Christian Ethics*, 235–46.

II

Engaging the Westphalian Idea of Sovereignty

6

Finding Common Ground in the Diversity of Civilizations

Looking Back, Looking Around

In the story of change in the conception of sovereignty told in the first part, we noted how two major challenges to consensus on the common ground provided by natural law led to an effort to locate a new common ground for morality and political life. That new common ground was found in the narrowing down of the inherited conception of natural law to focus on natural rights possessed by individuals and communities and, still further, to focus on the right of self-defense against harm or the threat of harm as the most basic natural right, one possessed universally. This change preserved, albeit at a very basic level, the idea of commonality among political communities: Whatever their differences, all agreed that each had the right to seek to protect and preserve itself. In the seventeenth century this provided a way for political communities to get along by at least not going to war over religious differences, and the global extension of this conception and the idea of state sovereignty defined by inviolate territorial borders has provided a base for the current international system.

But the changed idea of sovereignty did not come without cost: In practical terms, it opened the door to the rise of absolutism in individual states and to wars aimed at increasing territory or political dominion fought in the name of national defense. The latter has been addressed in contemporary international law through efforts aimed at preventing the first use of armed force in international disputes. Ironically, this has increased protection of absolutist governments who misuse their power and authority internally, oppressing and harming their own people or particular groups of them. This evil has been countered by the growth of human rights law and, specifically, the development of the doctrine of the responsibility to protect based on this law. In moral terms, the growth of human rights law proceeds from the acceptance of the common basic right of self-defense that lies at the base of the modern conception of sovereignty. It is an effort not only to reestablish a broader moral framework for understanding the relations of political communities and their governments between themselves but also to reestablish a common ground for conceiving of the actions of governments within their own societies in moral terms. Such a ground was lost when the broad premodern conception of natural law was discarded; the growth of human rights law is an effort to provide such a framework again on a different basis. Yet as we noted, broad consensus on human rights—what they are, where they come from, the priorities among the rights recognized, and so on—remains to be achieved. While there is substantial agreement that basic rights ought to be considered inviolate and generally protected, there is still disagreement on how to define those basic rights, both among the thinkers of various sorts who have offered their own definitions and listings and among the statements of such rights in authoritative international agreements. Moreover, in at least one particular arena where international law and custom have been established for a long time, the limits to be observed during armed conflict, one specific basic right, that of noncombatants not to be directly and intentionally attacked, has essentially been turned on its head in much contemporary armed conflict, where noncombatants are specifically targeted as a means of harming the enemy.

All this suggests that more attention should be paid to finding the kind of broader moral consensus that, in an earlier time, the conception of natural law provided within European culture. The enduring strength and possibilities for growth in the idea of naturally based human rights in Western culture serve as a reminder of the continuing effect of the underlying values of that earlier conception, even when the idea of natural law itself is not explicitly recognized or has become a bone of scholarly contention. But to recover more explicitly the sense of underlying common moral values in Western culture alone is not enough, for other major cultures and their civilizations also exist, and the larger problem is how to find a common ground that includes them. This is far from an insurmountable problem. As John Kelsay has observed, anyone who studies history is carrying out an investigation of different cultures from one's own. But that does not mean that it can be done casually or is easy to do well.[1]

One possibility is that no common ground can be found, that the global "clash of civilizations" must be either accepted as a continuing reality or else overcome with some new sort of hegemony. Samuel Huntington himself, who often has been read as arguing for the inevitability of intercivilizational conflict, actually offered a way toward avoiding such conflict, arguing that the West should "develop a more profound understanding of the basic religious and philosophical assumptions underlying other civilizations and the ways people in those civilizations see their interests," continuing that this "will require an effort to identify elements of commonality between Western and other civilizations."[2] In writing this, Huntington was specifically addressing the failure of Western political analysis and diplomats to seek such an understanding. But of course the argument for what the West should do also applies to other cultures or civilizations equally: The quest for such understanding needs to be mutual. Francis Fukuyama, explicitly taking note of the work of Huntington, though he is working from a Western scholarly perspective, offers an example of the kinds of knowledge and insights that may be gained through such a broader effort at understanding the world's major cultures and civilizations, their differences, and their commonalities.[3] His specific focus is the question of the origins of political order.[4] As I have noted elsewhere,[5] an earlier example of such an effort is provided specifically for the case of war across cultural and civilizational boundaries by the work of Quincy Wright.[6] In my own work I have sought to understand the nature, role, and transmission of moral values in the cultural regulation of violence,[7] and though my focus there was on Western culture and its history, I would argue for approaching other cultures similarly.[8]

In broad terms, I understand the problem posed by cultural or civilizational differences through the alternatives posed by Georg Schwarzenberger, who was thinking specifically of the case of international law, in *The Frontiers of International Law*: consensus, reciprocity, or hegemony.[9] For Schwarzenberger, "community law" proceeds from a general consensus as to values and serves to promulgate those values, interpret them, and coordinate various elements of custom and perspective in understanding them and their application to life. What Schwarzenberger calls "law" refers not simply to positive legislation but to broadly held cultural understandings and their institutional expressions. The second alternative identified by Schwarzenberger is the "law of reciprocity," in which communities formed around different understandings of value define a way to interact by trading off inferior values and the institutions and behaviors associated with them in order to protect and preserve higher values and their cultural expressions. The third alternative is the "law of hegemony," in which commonality, at least in forms of behavior, is imposed by the domination of one community over others.

Western Europe prior to the Reformation enjoyed a general consensus as to values and organized social and political behavior accordingly. The Protestant-Catholic divide brought about as a result of the Reformation expressed a new division on the values associated specifically with religion, though other values (the majority by far) continued to be held in common. The state system set in place by the Peace of Westphalia built on the older "community law" but introduced a new pattern of relationship framed in terms of reciprocity, as the parties agreed to allow each one to govern itself internally as it pleased (in particular through the decision as to the established religion) but not to seek to impose its own determination on others by force. This latter was reinforced by the new understanding of sovereignty as territorial inviolability and the right of defense as a fundamental right held by all political communities.

Outside Europe the patterns differed. Relations with the Turkish Empire were characterized by a mix of reciprocal interactions and efforts by one side or the other to dominate the other hegemonically. Trading relations with other parts of the world began in the form of an organized reciprocity, but this changed to hegemonic relations first in the conquest, settlement, and fortification of centers designed to support trade and exploration, and then over time in the imperial hegemonic domination of larger areas and their inhabitants. The Spanish interaction with the New World very quickly took on this latter pattern, and as other European societies began their own interactions with the New World, they followed suit. The imperial regime facilitated the spread of European values, institutions, and modes of behavior to the colonized areas and their inhabitants. This took place by a variety of means, and its success or failure varied from region to region. The spread of Roman Catholic Christianity was an integral part of Spanish colonization of the New World almost from the very beginning; similarly the spread of Russian imperialism carried Orthodox Christianity, and later it carried Communism, as did Chinese imperial extension. The nineteenth-century American expansion into the Pacific mixed the purposes of trade and Protestant Christian missionizing (described by one commentator as the effort to bring "light to the gentiles by means of lamps manufactured in America");[10] more recently the spread of American influence (if not colonization) has been represented in terms of spreading democracy. In the nineteenth century and early twentieth the French and Portuguese described their purposes in their African colonies with the phrase "civilizing mission," and British imperial policy in various ways aimed to establish the English language and English institutions in the parts of the empire. [11] As late as 1962, in the book by Schwarzenberger already cited, he spoke of international law as carrying and imposing the principles of "civilization." In another widely influential book on international order published at about the same time, Myres S. McDougal and Florentino P. Feliciano spoke of international law as establishing the principle of "humanity" or "humanitarianism,"[12] where despite the word change from Schwarzenberger, the sense was much the same: Here was a value established in Western culture that was being exported to the rest of the world by means of international law.

The wave of imperial hegemony has passed, though of course hegemony persists in other forms. In the international order, though, it has given way, at least in theory, to a consensus expressed in international law (though, when examined closely, international law more accurately expresses a mixture of consensus, continued cultural hegemony, and trade-offs typically expressed as withheld consent to certain provisions of certain international agreements). The shifting purposes, abilities, and power relationships in the world have allowed for the reassertion of the values of other major world cultures and the civilizations rooted in them, and as a result the problem of understanding, organizing, and managing the relationships among them has become more serious. Is there to be some new effort at hegemony (for example, that of radical Islamism or, in a narrower geographic frame, that of China in the western pacific)? Will the relationships take the form of cross-cultural toleration, if not acceptance, coupled with various forms of trade-offs tailored to the needs and abilities of the parties? Or is some higher level of consensus and community to be found?

To attempt to say yes to this last alternative rests on the possibility that there are indeed common values and assumptions that transcend civilizational and cultural lines, and that these constitute a common ground that can be built on productively. To explore this possibility in certain specific ways, focusing particularly on the question of the understanding of sovereignty with regard to responsible rule, is the work of this chapter.

To carry out this exploration is to take a road not taken in the earlier "clashes of civilizations" of the early modern period that led to reconceiving first the basis and then the idea of sovereignty during the sixteenth and seventeenth centuries: to look for common values and conceptions in the competing value systems and institutions. I will look particularly at relevant elements in a cultural system that has produced major challenges to the values and institutions of the West: that of resurgent Islam in the form of militant Islamic radicalism.

Why focus on the case of Islam? There are several reasons. First, Islamic culture is by any reckoning one of the world's major cultures, though it is relatively new. It is effectively defined by the historic spread of the religion of Islam and its influence on the existing cultures of the regions in which Islam took root; thus today it encompasses a broad geographic area that stretches from North Africa and sub-Saharan Africa eastward to present-day Indonesia, including most of the Middle East, Asia Minor, parts of Central Asia, Afghanistan, and parts of the Indian subcontinent. Its distinctive political and social expression was the Abbasid caliphate centered on Baghdad, but it also produced other caliphates in areas distant from that seat of power and three major empires, the Turkish, the Persian, and the Mughul in India. Because of the central Islamic doctrine that the Qur'an is the literal record of the divine revelation in its final form, the spread of the religion of Islam also meant the spread of the Arabic language and literacy in it. In its early centuries, owing importantly to this emphasis on literacy, the absorption and preservation of classical Greek and Roman thought, and the wealth and power of several of the regional political communities that developed, Islamic culture excelled in science, philosophy, architecture, and other fields of human endeavor. That it was early recognized as a common culture is testified to by the example of the *Muqaddimah*, a pioneering work of universal history and philosophy of history written in the latter part of the fourteenth century (seventh century AH), whose author, Ibn Khaldun, traveled from his home in the Maghreb across North Africa and into the Middle East, taking note approvingly of the common religion, language, modes of thought, and patterns of life he encountered throughout his journey. So one reason to examine the case of Islamic culture here is simply its importance as a major world culture.

A second reason, especially important for the question of whether common ground can be found across cultures, is the challenge to Western culture in all its forms posed by the radical Islamist interpretation of the religion of Islam and its meaning for the faithful. In the West this contemporary form of Islam is perhaps most usually associated with terrorist attacks against civilians and against the structures of civilian life itself. However, it has also been deeply involved in military conflict, ranging from Iraq and Afghanistan to the war to overthrow the regime of the Syrian President Bashar al-Assad, and in efforts to reshape political life, as seen in different forms in Iran after the revolution that overthrew the Shah, in Afghanistan under the Taliban, and in the emergence of conservative Islamist political movements all across the Islamic world. The challenge thus posed strikes directly at the idea of finding common ground across cultures, as radical Islamism defines its mission (and that of the religion of Islam) as hegemony over the world as a whole.

The third reason for concentrating on the case of Islamic culture here is that this is where my own work outside of the frame of Western culture has focused. Following Huntington's observation as to learning about other cultures or civilizations as a way to avoid armed conflict across cultural and civilizational lines, I have been working to understand elements of Islamic religion and culture for over the last two decades. Looking for commonalities requires a serious level of knowledge of both cultures being examined. Thus I start where my own knowledge lies.

In the following discussion I focus first on the Islamic tradition on good government, both the theory and the practice, including the expectations of the good ruler and the place of the use of force in the exercise of such government; I then turn to present-day radical Islamism on these topics. Last, I offer an assessment of where common ground lies and the challenge to it posed by radical Islamism.

Islamic Conceptions Defining Good Government

While various contemporary states, including such diverse examples as Iran and Pakistan, describe themselves as having "Islamic" governments, there is no consensus as to what the nature of such a government would be or how it would relate to other states within the existing international order. Both sectarian differences among Muslims and differences shaped by the particular historical experiences of particular Muslim-majority societies militate against the coalescence of any such consensus today. Yet there is a rich tradition of thought on the proper shape of a genuinely Islamic society and its government to which diverse political movements in the contemporary world have appealed in different ways. The following section examines the tradition of Islamic thought on good government and the somewhat different ways this tradition was interpreted in political practice, while the subsequent section focuses on the way recent radical Islamism has interpreted the earlier tradition for its own purposes.

The Tradition: Theory and Practice

The basic principles of Islamic thought and practice on political community and its government were established during the lifetime of the Prophet Muhammad, which for Islam is also the period in which the Qur'an, the written record of the final form of God's revelation to humanity, was given. Most fundamental was the religious principle of *tawhid*, "unity," laid down in the Qur'an and given expression in the opening lines of the Muslim confession of faith ("There is no God but God, and Muhammad is his prophet"). This was reflected in the organization of the Muslim community, which was understood and developed as simultaneously a political unit and one religiously defined by reference to the divine revelation, and in its leadership by a single person understood as bearing final authority in both political (including military) and religious matters. Originally this one person was the Prophet Muhammad himself; after his death, the principle of unity in the community continued, as did the principle of leadership by a single man, described as the successor or deputy (*khalifa*, "caliph") of the Prophet. The first major controversy in the Islamic community was over who might legitimately hold this role, the inheritor of the prophet's authority in the community: Did the successor need to be of the prophet's bloodline, or should he be the person judged to be the most worthy overall, regardless of bloodline? Initially the decision was for the latter, and the first three caliphs (Abu Bakr, Umar, and Uthman) were chosen on the basis of judgment as to this criterion. But the accession of the fourth caliph, Ali, the prophet's grandson, reignited the smoldering controversy over legitimate leadership in succession to the prophet, with the supporters of ᶜAli known as the *shiᶜat ᶜAli*, the "Party of Ali," shortened to *shiᶜa*. Ali was murdered in

661 (39 AH), giving rise to civil war within the Muslim community over his successor. This war ended with the Battle of Karbala in 680 (58 AH), when Husayn, the prophet's grandson, and other members of the Party of Ali were killed. After this, Shi^c^ism continued as a religious movement, and in certain areas it also gained political power, but the mainstream of Islam developed differently, in regard to both religion and political organization. The victorious caliph, Mu^c^awiyya, who succeeded Ali, went on to found the first caliphal dynasty, the Umayyad, while the Shi^c^a retreated into grudging submission. The Umayyads presided over the initial wave of Islamic expansion westward across North Africa and into Spain, as well as eastward as far as the northern parts of the Indian subcontinent. The Umayyads increasingly emphasized the political side of their rule, and in the first part of the eighth century (second century AH) a reaction against this began, which resulted in the overthrow of the Umayyads (in 750 [128 AH]) in the core Islamic lands and the establishment of a new caliphal dynasty, the Abbasid, whose appeal, over against the Umayyads, included the expectation that they would restore the place of religion in the government of the Islamic community.

It was under the early Abbasids, and with their favor, that the jurisprudential or legal understanding of the religion of Islam took root, with the founding of the four major schools (*madhabs*) of Islamic jurisprudence (*fiqh*). Two of the major jurists of this period, al-Shaybani (of the Hanafi school, founded not long before him by Ibn Hanifa) and al-Shafi^c^i (the founder of the school that bears his name), established, in juristic form, a theoretical understanding of the Islamic state, its jointly political and religious character, its governance according to divinely revealed law (*shari^c^a*) by a caliph, heir to the supreme religious and political authority of the Prophet Muhammad. They defined the Islamic state as the territory ruled by such a ruler on the basis of Islamic law; they called it the *dar al-islam* (literally "the gate of Islam," usually translated as the "abode" or "house" of Islam), setting it over against all the different sorts of communities of the remainder of the world, calling them collectively the *dar al-harb* (the "abode" or "house" of war) because, in their not being ruled according to the express will of God by a ruler with legitimate authority, they were prone to strife and warfare both within and among themselves and between them (as a group and as individual entities) and the *dar al-islam*. In this conception warfare with the *dar al-harb* was understood as inevitable, because of the latter's character; throughout history the *dar al-islam* would need to engage in striving (*jihad*) against it, both by spiritual means and by the sword. Only at the end of time would this opposition cease, with the *dar al-islam* encompassing the whole of humankind.

This juristic conception provided a powerful religious and intellectual undergirding to the establishment of the Abbasid caliphate, its subsequent history, and its claim to universal jurisdiction over the entire world of Islam. It has remained as the guiding normative conception for Islamic political order, and it provides the basis, as will be shown below, for present-day radical Islamist thinking about political order. A similar doctrine, also described in juristic terms, developed within Shi^c^ism, where the caliphs were rejected as "unjust rulers" and the leader who was regarded as the legitimate heir to the authority of the Prophet Muhammad was termed the Imam, a title that emphasized his religious authority over the political.

Yet the early Abbasid jurists' conception of a single universal Islamic territory ruled according to Islamic law by a single ruler in the heritage of the Prophet Muhammad never became historical fact outside the core Abbasid area, even as the theory was first being expounded not only as a normative statement for how the Muslim community ought to be organized but as a description of the relations between Muslims and the non-Muslim world. Some relevant dates will help to illustrate this. First, al-Shaybani and al-Shafi^c^i both lived and wrote in the latter part of the eighth century and the beginning of the ninth, the former dying in 805, the latter in 820. Their writings established the juristic conception described above. In the sphere of political life, the Abbasid dynasty began in 750, but though it displaced the Umayyads in the core Islamic lands, six years later, in 756, its claim to universal rule was challenged by an Umayyad *amir* (commander) who established himself as an independent ruler in Cordova, Spain. In 788 another independent dynasty (the Idrisid) was established in Morocco, in 799–800 another (the Aghlabid) in Tunisia. The rulers in these three areas ruled independently from the caliph in Baghdad, hundreds of miles and weeks of travel away, though they did not adopt the title caliph for themselves at first. In 910, however, the Fatimid dynasty established itself as a rival caliphate in North Africa, and in 929 the ruler of Cordova also adopted the title of caliph. In 932 another dynasty, the Buwahid, was established in Persia, which before had been, at least nominally, ruled by the caliph in Baghdad.

After this, the pattern of independent Muslim states, with their rulers sometimes bearing the title caliph and sometimes not, continued as the historical reality, whatever the power of the juristic normative conception in defining the ideal of Muslim religio-political order as a unity governed by a single ruler, heir to the authority of the Prophet Muhammad, according to divinely revealed law. The Baghdad caliphate itself ended as a source of ruling power with the fall of Baghdad to the Mongol invasion in 1258, though successive members of the Abbasid dynasty continued to bear the title of caliph and remained at least a symbolic center of both religious and political authority. By the time Baghdad fell, though, significant parts of the Abbasid territory had fallen to Christian forces and subsequent rulers as a result of the Crusades, and a new center of practical power and authority emerged in Asia Minor, the Ottoman Sultanate (established in 1299). The authority remaining in the Abbasid caliphate was absorbed into the political hegemony of the Ottoman state during the reign of Selim I (Sultan 1512–20), who brought the last of the Abbasid line, the caliph al-Mutawwakil, to his capital and, after the latter's death, claimed that he had given the title of caliph and its authority to Selim and his successors. After this, the Ottoman rulers could claim universal jurisdiction as heirs to the caliphate, but independent centers of power still continued to exist, drawing as useful on the ideal conception defined in the juristic tradition.

Returning to this ideal conception, what was the conception of sovereignty and its right exercised there? First of all, ultimate sovereignty over the entire created world was understood as belonging to God. Muhammad had been the messenger or prophet of God, but his authority as a religious and political leader was delegated from God. Similarly, the legitimacy of subsequent leaders depended on their being regarded as successors to this delegated authority and on their fealty to the revealed law of God, understood as a complete guide for human affairs. Not an alien imposition, this law was understood as spelling out what is already implanted in human nature by God, so that living according to it is living in accord with our inner nature as created by God. The good life is thus one of *islam*, which means "submission." The caliph's focal obligation in his rule was to govern the *dar al-islam* by this revealed law and to seek to spread the rule of this law into the areas "without the law," the *dar al-harb*. By doing so, he brings the people thus governed into behavior in accord with their own inner good. But first, the caliph had the personal obligation of accepting this law and living in accord with it. Success in this would carry over into success in his broader rule.

Islamic culture thus also has at its core a conception of the exercise of government (though described not as "sovereignty" but as *khilafa*, "deputy-ship") as responsibility for the common good. This understanding is not limited to the juristic tradition but also took the form of the idea of the "virtuous ruler" in the Muslim philosophical tradition, in which the earliest major figure is al-Farabi (870–950 [257–339 AH]), who lived and wrote not long after the beginnings of the juristic tradition. In looking briefly at his thought I follow the analysis of Charles Butterworth.

Unlike the jurists, al-Farabi drew not only on Islamic revelation but on the classical philosophical thought of Greece and Rome, emphasizing the right use of reason, rather than revelation understood as law, as the way to understand the divine will as expressed in nature. For him the goal of the virtuous ruler is "only to obtain, for himself and for everyone under his rulership, the ultimate happiness that is truly happiness."[13] To the end of guiding the ruler in doing this, the philosopher should employ the science of politics or political science, which differs from religion in the following way: "Whereas virtuous religion is concerned with what the citizens need to believe and to do in order to obtain ultimate happiness, political science is concerned with investigating and then explaining what the virtuous ruler needs to think and do in order to help the citizens obtain ultimate happiness."[14] But political science understood in this way operates as a function of right religion; it is the use of reason to explore what religion requires. There is also, for al-Farabi, a kind of political science that is part of philosophy alone, which focuses on universals and does not address the praxis of virtuous rule.

The exercise of virtuous rule includes the waging of justified war, war with the purpose of justice, though his list of justifications goes beyond the definition of just cause in Western just war tradition, and includes a justification that corresponds to one given by the jurists for offensive jihad of the sword against some portion of the *dar al-harb*: "carrying and forcing a certain people to what is best and most fortunate for them, . . . when they have not known it on their own and have not submitted to someone who knows it and calls them to it by speech."[15] In this context al-Farabi does not use the word "jihad," which denotes "striving" in the path of God; as he presents it, this justification is part of the exercise of virtue able to be known by the use of reason. Elsewhere, though, when talking about the "fighters" or "guardians" who both carry out such warfare and protect the virtuous city from attackers, he calls them *mujahidun* and employs the term "jihad" for both of these kinds of warfare,[16] a usage corresponding to that of the jurists.

Justified warfare, though, is only one aspect of the exercise of virtuous rule and is defined by the larger goal described above: to lead those under the ruler's care to their ultimate happiness, an idea from classical Greek and Roman thought and preserved in the just war tradition and its idea of sovereignty as their "good" or "end." Though al-Farabi comes to his understanding of this, as do the jurists, through the religion of Islam, both he and they conceive of this as in accord with human nature itself. This is in fact an understanding similar to natural law in Western tradition, where the *ius naturale* is also understood as an expression of the divine *ius*. The two traditions also share a common problem, though: how to maintain this higher understanding without at the same time insisting that it must be approached through the particular statement of it provided by the specific religious tradition.

Radical Islamism's Use of the Tradition

The movement in contemporary Islamic societies that I here call "radical Islamism" has been called by a variety of names, this among them.[17] It is the option I prefer because of the meaning of the term "radical," referring to an effort to reach back to the roots of Islam, a claim at the core of this movement. Despite this claim, though, historically and doctrinally this movement is associated with reformist efforts in both Sunni and Shi^ca Islam from the late eighteenth century and early nineteenth, efforts closely tied to resistance against outside domination by colonial and imperial powers. In Iran this took the form of the involvement of the *ᶜulama* (the learned clergy) in offering religious arguments supporting resistance against foreign intruders, first the Russians, then the British, and, in the case of the Iranian Revolution under the Ayatollah Khomeini, against the perceived foreign domination of the Shah and his government and, more generally, against the growth of Western cultural influences in the country. In the Indian subcontinent it took the form of various specific efforts aimed at asserting the historical mission of Islam to establish rule by *shariᶜa*, first against the British, then against the Hindu-dominated Indian state after independence, and then against Western influences in the government of Pakistan. In Afghanistan the Taliban effort to establish an Islamic state ruled according to the provisions of *shariᶜa* drew from this history. But perhaps the most important root of present-day radical Islamism is the influence of the Wahhabi movement, so called from the name of its founder, Muhammad ibn ᶜabd al-Wahhab (1703–91), who in the mid-eighteenth century drew together a group of scholars who began to issue opinions on *shariᶜa* condemning much of the practice of Islam as it then existed in the place Islam had originated, the Arabian peninsula. In 1746 ibn ᶜabd al-Wahhab formed an alliance with the al-Saᶜud family, drawing the latter into his campaign against this widespread "heedlessness" and using the al-Saᶜud military power to enforce the Wahhabi understanding of the requirements of true Islam. This led to the founding of the Saudi state, with Wahhabi Islam serving as its undergirding ideology. The influence of the Wahhabi understanding of Islam is deep and widespread in the most militant forms of radical Islamism and is seen particularly in al-Qaeda.

John Kelsay in a recent study examines what he prefers to call "militant Islam" or "Islamic militancy" as it exists today through three documents: the "creed of Sadat's assassins," known in English as *The Neglected Duty*, written in 1981, the Charter of Hamas from 1988, and *The Declaration on Armed Struggle against Jews and Crusaders* issued in 1998 by a group of leaders of various radical Islamist organizations styling themselves the World Islamic Front, whose members included Osama bin Ladin, already the leader of al-Qaeda, and Ayman al-Zawahiri, later to become bin Ladin's deputy but then the head of the militant branch of the Muslim Brotherhood in Egypt.[18] For our purposes here, with our focus on the question of the meaning of sovereignty, the most important of these is *The Neglected Duty*.[19]

The title of this work refers to the duty of Muslims to establish an Islamic state,[20] which is to be a territorial nucleus from which a revived universal caliphate can be established. Such a state would be ruled by the laws of Islam,[21] and by a ruler who governs according to these laws.[22] For the author of this work, "The Rulers of this age are in apostasy from Islam. They were raised at the tables of imperialism, be it Crusaderism, or Communism, or Zionism,"[23] and they govern not by Islamic law but by "other (mere human) opinions, ideas, and conventions, that were made by humans who had no recourse to the Law of God."[24] He goes on to compare these contemporary rulers with the Mongols, who after overthrowing the

Abbasid Caliphate in 1258 set up their own rule in its place, professing themselves to be Muslims but not following Islamic law.[25] In connection with the Mongols the document's focus shifts to the Hanbali jurist Ibn Taymiyyah, who wrote in reaction to them. Ibn Taymiyyah's understanding of Islamic law thus becomes the standard for the meaning of behavior in accord with this law in a time of crisis due to apostasy from the law. How to fight against apostate rulers and those who side with them? The answer is not by political means, by the building up of a majority: "Islam does not triumph by attracting (the support of) the majority."[26] Such rulers and those who take part with them must be killed, and any Muslim who dies in battle against them is a martyr.[27] In short, to fight against such rulers is a religious duty, and doing so is a form of jihad. Such jihad is thus obligatory for all genuine Muslims; each has this obligation as an individual duty.[28] At this point *The Neglected Duty* returns to the matter of the obligation to establish an Islamic state, describing such establishment as "the execution of a divine command."[29] Jihad, first introduced in connection with the obligation to remove the apostate rulers and those who side with them, is now presented as the way to the establishment of the Islamic state, the state ruled according to the law of God by a ruler who is obedient to that law,[30] and the neglect of jihad in this connection becomes another aspect of "the neglected duty" to which the title of the document refers.[31] The remainder of the document focuses on how this jihad is to be fought, including the obligatory religious cleanness that warriors in its ranks must observe, described as "complete devotion to the cause of God."[32]

For *The Neglected Duty* the ideal state is one that is ruled by Islamic law, *shari^ca*; no other law is to be allowed, as we have seen, because it is only human "opinions, ideas, and conventions," and God's law takes precedence over them. Good rule consists in the enforcement of this law throughout the state's territory, and because the way to a state constituted and governed in this way is by jihad of the sword waged by those (understood to be a minority) who personally embody obedience to this law, the leader in this jihad, the one recognized as supreme in leading the faithful in the fulfillment of their obligation, is the one who also has the qualities to rule the Islamic state once it has been established.

There is also no room for an appeal to natural law regarding this conception. Though Islamic tradition describes the revealed law as what is natural to everyone, there is no discussion of this relationship here.

Rather, depending on the "natural" is explicitly rejected, since God can and will change that if he wishes: "A Muslim has first of all the duty to execute the command to fight with his hands. (Once he has done so) God . . . will then intervene (and change) the laws of nature."[33] God's will is supreme over nature, and divine action can change nature. But the revealed law of God does not change. Thus it is the only basis that can be allowed for guiding human behavior, the only law that can be allowed for an Islamic state.

The idea of sovereignty defined here is thus defined religiously, and moreover, by a particular line of interpretation of what is religiously required. Divinely given law—the "law of Islam," "God's law"—provides an absolute standard for the nature of the state and the way it is governed. It is interesting that the establishment of such a state, which must be achieved through the waging of jihad, is described as a first step toward the reestablishment of the universal caliphate. This distinction allows for a distinction in the way the ruling authority is described. Leadership in the jihad necessary to found the truly Islamic state belongs to the one recognized as leader because of his fidelity to the law and his ability to lead his followers to the desired goal. The exercise of sovereign rule within the Islamic state, once it is established, thus appears to be an extension of the leadership in the jihad that brings it into being. This is a rather different conception from that of leadership in the Islamic community defined early in Islamic tradition, as we have seen it. There, while fealty to the revealed law is a necessary characteristic of the ruler, and while the rule of the *dar al-islam*, the territory of Islam, is to follow the divinely revealed law, the person chosen for this is defined as a "deputy" or "successor" (the meaning of *khalifa*, "caliph") to the Prophet Muhammad and an inheritor of his authority in both religious and temporal matters. *The Neglected Duty* does not describe the leadership in the jihad necessary to establish an Islamic state, or the leadership of that state itself once established, in this way. The authority to rule is not described as an inheritance of the authority of the prophet, but rather comes from fidelity to the law and superiority in achieving the ends desired. Possibly the authority and responsibility of the caliph, once a caliphate is reestablished, would be described in the terms of the earlier tradition, but the scope of *The Neglected Duty* is the struggle for the establishment of the Islamic state that is not yet the caliphate, though it is understood as a necessary prerequisite to it.

It is far from clear that any of the historical Muslim states, even those that understood themselves as caliphates, would pass the test for the genuinely Islamic state described in *The Neglected Duty*. Certainly there would be no room in this state for disagreements on the meaning of the law itself or on the behavior it requires. Strict conformity would need to be enforced on all Muslims, with nonconformists in danger of being treated as if they were in apostasy from Islam and thus subject to the death penalty. Non-Muslim inhabitants of this ideal Islamic state would be on an extremely short leash as regards both behavior and thought. Certainly there could be no place for philosophical reflection aimed at understanding natural law and relating it to the revealed law. And even juristic interpretation would have its limits, for the "vanity of a Man of Religion" makes him subject to the ruler or commander in jihad and in the state.[34] A state based on any form of Shiʿa Islam would not meet the test; nor would one based on, say, a Sufi tradition of interpretation of the law; nor would a relatively open and tolerant (and highly successful) state like the Andalusian Caliphate; nor would a state such as the Ottoman Empire, because of its division of government into temporal and religious spheres and its development of laws and practices in the former sphere not specifically grounded in the religious law.

Conclusion: Common Ground or Necessary Enmity?

Following Georg Schwarzenberger's description of the three possible kinds of law, I suggested that there are three basic alternatives for relations across cultures or civilizations: community, or finding common ground that transcends the differences between them; reciprocity, or developing ways of getting along involving the willingness and ability of each of the cultures or civilizations to define a workable way of getting along by a mutual exchange of values, that is, giving up on some preferences deemed of lesser value in order to reach agreement or at least toleration on preferences of greater value; or hegemony, in which the values of one culture or civilization are imposed on the rest by one means or another. The first of these is the form of law in cohesive political communities, as well as between various political communities where there is broad agreement on the values to be served. The second describes well the model of contemporary positive international law (though elements of the first and third options can be found there too), which is defined by the decision of the powers to construct the law in a certain way; the reservations listed at the end of international agreements signal points where specific parties hold to positions expressing values that they wish to maintain with no diminution. The third is historically exemplified by imperial cultures, though on close look at the majority of cases, one also observes a considerable degree of acceptance of local community law and working arrangements built on reciprocal interactions. The hegemony may be military, political, economic, religious, linguistic, or other, or it may be mixed. The results appear different in each case.

While significant common ground on basic values, apart from their specific intellectual or institutional expression, can be found between Western culture and Islamic culture, and while mutually beneficial reciprocal interactions have come into being not only in international law but in international relations more broadly, and while there has been widespread voluntary adoption of Western mores and related values within Islamic societies, the example of *The Neglected Duty* provides a case in which there is a fundamental "clash of civilizations" between the culture of Islam and other cultures, whether of "Crusaderism, or Communism, or Zionism," to recall language quoted. Any possibility of commonality, as well as any pattern of interaction expressing a mixture of values from other cultures, is explicitly and vehemently rejected. In this case, then, the possibility of working to find common ground is taken off the table from the start, whatever those possibilities may seem to be when the deeper cultural traditions are examined.

The same would, of course, be the case with other examples of a similar sort. In recent history such examples would include the case of the Nazis and of the Marxist-Leninist ideology of the Soviet Union. At the beginning of the modern period, the Spanish colonization of the New World proceeded with a similarly all-or-nothing conception of Christianity and Spanish culture at its base. During the wars of religion in the century after the beginnings of the Reformation, both sides, working from their own certainty of being in the right, demonized each other. These were the sorts of realities that the new conception of sovereignty in terms of inviolable territory and its defense, plus the state system built on this conception, sought to correct.

Among the important implications to be drawn from reflection not only on radical Islamism but also on other cases such as these is that in the international realm the conception of sovereignty as having to do fundamentally with the defense of territory against all others, while leaving no room for others to have any say in how a government behaves inside its own territorial borders, continues to serve well. Where the foundation of an ideal Islamic state, as described in *The Neglected Duty*, is concerned, there is no room in this conception of sovereignty for the expansion of such a state across the border into the territory of any state that does not share the Islamic state's fundamental values and mode of government. But inside its own borders, it may reject any outside pressure to govern differently. Afghanistan under the Taliban is the best historical example of such a result.

But the radical understanding of Islam and of the construction of political societies according to the requirements of Islam remains a minority position, not only in the world as a whole but within Islamic culture itself. The diversity within the world of Islam suggests that there is a future for the possibility of finding common ground, whatever the projihad radicals may hold. The best test for this may be the outcome of the political changes brought by the revolutions of the "Arab Spring," which at this writing have been different in each of the societies affected, though the results have not yet completely stabilized. And then, of course, there remains the question of how the other cultures of the world develop in themselves and in their attitudes toward one another, and in their reactions to the changes brought by the revolutions of the "Arab Spring." The search for community and the search for reciprocity both require the participation of all the concerned parties. In the context of the question being examined in the present book—the question of whether some commonality can be found across the cultures of the world that would allow for the restoration of a conception of sovereignty as responsibility for the common good—the answer remains unresolved.

Notes

1. Kelsay, "Just War, Jihad, and the Study of Comparative Ethics," 227–38.
2. Huntington, "The Clash of Civilizations?," 22–49.
3. Fukuyama, *The Origins of Political Order.*
4. Ibid.
5. Johnson, *Just War Tradition and the Restraint of War,* (1981), 41–44; Johnson, *The Holy War Idea in Western and Islamic Traditions*, 5.
6. Wright, *A Study of War*, 155–56.

7. Johnson, *Just War Tradition*, chaps. 3, 4.
8. As in Johnson, *Holy War Idea*, chap. 1.
9. Schwarzenberger, *The Frontiers of International Law*, chap. 1.
10. Niebuhr, *The Kingdom of God in America*, 179.
11. For a recent detailed effort to tell the full story of England's relationship to its empire, see Niall Ferguson's suggestively titled *Civilization*.
12. McDougal and Feliciano, *Law and Minimum World Public Order*, 71ff.
13. Al-Farabi, quoted in Butterworth, "Al-Farabi's Statecraft: War and the Well-Ordered Regime," 79–100.
14. Ibid., 82.
15. Al-Farabi, ibid., 84.
16. Ibid., 87.
17. For a sampling, see Wright, *A Study of War*; Kelsay, *Arguing the Just War in Islam*, 2.
18. Kelsay, *Arguing the Just War*, 129–49.
19. Jansen, *The Neglected Duty*.
20. Section 16; ibid., 165–66.
21. Section 18; ibid., 166.
22. Section 21; ibid., 167.
23. Section 25; ibid.
24. Section 25; ibid., 169.
25. Sections 29–35; ibid., 172–75.
26. Section 55; ibid., 186.
27. Section 43; ibid., 179–80.
28. Sections 68–72; ibid., 192–94; sections 84–87: ibid., 199–200.
29. Section 91; ibid., 201–2.
30. Sections 92–99; ibid., 202–5.
31. Sections 100–102; ibid., 205–7.
32. Section 130; ibid., 222.
33. Section 65; ibid., 190.
34. Sections 140–43; ibid., 229–30.

7

The Two Conceptions of Sovereignty and the "Responsibility to Protect" Doctrine

Introduction: The Background

We have been examining two conceptions of sovereignty. To summarize: The one that held sway from the high Middle Ages till the seventeenth century was defined in terms of the responsibility of the sovereign authority for the common good of the people governed and for maintaining relations among political communities that support the sovereigns' discharge of this responsibility; the other, which began to develop in thought about just war in the sixteenth century and effectively replaced the older conception in Grotius's thought and in the political system based on the Peace of Westphalia, was based on a minimal conception of human rights as the right of self-defense against attack and built from that a conception of sovereignty defined in terms of the territorial integrity and inviolability of each political community, with ruling authority delegated upward from the people of each such community and understood as having the primary responsibility of defending its territory.

The older conception had lost force because of the challenges to a sense of common moral ground posed first by the encounter with the New World and then more forcefully by the division of European society along religious lines as a result of the Reformation, a division that manifested itself in a century of grossly destructive warfare over religion. The new conception of sovereignty aimed importantly at preventing wars over rival religious belief, but while it succeeded in this aim (though in the last century it has not prevented conflicts inflamed by secular ideologies—a functional equivalent to religion—and by the rise of militant radical Islamism), it also provided a ground for two unforeseen and undesirable new developments: the initiation of war by governments of their own choosing on the grounds of the defense of national territory and, through the principle of noninterference in the internal affairs of any state, the ability of governments to treat the people governed however they wished, free from outside interference. This second development in particular reflected the new definition of sovereignty in which general responsibility for the common good was reduced to responsibility for self-defense against attack, with this in turn defined as ultimately located in each individual. The problem, then, has been how to restore the idea that government has such a broad responsibility while maintaining the new definition of sovereignty in the minimalist terms of maintaining territorial integrity against external attack.

Efforts to constrain the initiation of war to the choice of ruling authorities—the so-called *liberum jus ad bellum*—included the use of balance-of-power alliances, stress on arbitration as a means of settling international differences in the League of Nations Covenant, and the effort to outlaw by mutual consent of nations the first resort to armed force in any international dispute, first put in place by the Pact of Paris (Kellogg-Briand Pact) of 1928 and then made part of the United Nations Charter. The second problem—abuses of some parts or all of their populations by the governing authorities themselves or by others without being checked by government—was for a long time tolerated, not being regarded as a matter for international agreements or action. After the Second World War, however, this began to change, with the development of the doctrine of "the responsibility to protect" early in the present century importantly a result of changes in international law initiated shortly after the end of the war and the creation of the United Nations.

The first of these changes was the establishment of international legal trials for the identification and punishment of war crimes at the end of the war. The Nuremberg Principles, developed in connection with the trials in that city, provided the first legal definition of war crimes not only as violations of specific international agreements in the laws of war but as "crimes against humanity."[1] This concept of crimes against humanity represented an effort to recover and restate basic elements of a moral consensus as to the right treatment owed to people in general as a result of their common humanity. This idea has provided a broad context within which subsequent international law on armed conflict has evolved, but it has also done so for the specific case of the prohibition of genocide and the broader case of the development of human rights law.

The second major change was the adoption by the United Nations General Assembly of the Convention on the Prevention and Punishment of the Crime of Genocide (the Genocide Convention) on December 9, 1948.[2] While the Nazis' treatment of Jews and other minority groups during World War II provided the specific background for the development and adoption of this convention, it provided a broad definition of genocide as "a crime under international law," which could cover any new cases of similar oppression:

> Article II. In the present Convention, genocide means any of the following acts committed with intent to destroy, in whole or in part, a national, ethnical, racial or religious group, as such:
>
> (a) Killing members of the group;
>
> (b) Causing serious bodily or mental harm to members of the group;
>
> (c) Deliberately inflicting on the group conditions of life calculated to bring about its physical destruction in whole or in part;
>
> (d) Imposing measures intended to prevent births within the group;
>
> (e) Forcibly transferring children of the group to another group.

What was lacking in the convention itself was provision for its enforcement; this was left to "the Contracting Parties" (Article V). The definition of genocide, though, provided an important statement of a moral floor to the treatment of members of any of the kinds of groups named.

On the day after the adoption of the Genocide Convention, the General Assembly adopted another statement of basic principles, The Universal Declaration of Human Rights.[3] This, together with the other two documents noted above, marks the beginning of the development of human rights law as a distinct category in international law. Again, this declaration established an important moral floor, though the subsequent development of human rights law has introduced elements of confusion and tension as to just what human rights are, the priorities among them, and how they should be protected.

Also relevant in the present connection is the post–World War II development of a distinctive branch of international law already well established prior to the war: the law of war or, as it has subsequently come to be known, the law of armed conflicts. Common Article 3 of the Geneva Conventions of 1949 laid down basic rules for the treatment of civilians (defined as "persons taking no active part in the hostilities," normally referred to in moral thought as noncombatants) as a category;

these provisions were subsequently reaffirmed as applying to both international and noninternational armed conflicts by the 1977 Protocols to these Conventions.[4] Common Article 3 reads in part as follows:

> Persons taking no active part in the hostilities . . . shall in all circumstances be treated humanely, without any adverse distinction founded on race, colour, religion or faith, sex, birth or wealth, or any other similar criteria.
>
> To this end the following acts are and shall remain prohibited: . . .
>
> (a) violence to life and person, in particular murder of all kinds, mutilation, cruel treatment and torture;
>
> (b) taking of hostages;
>
> (c) outrages upon personal dignity, in particular humiliating and degrading treatment;
>
> (d) the passing of sentences and the carrying out of executions without previous judgment pronounced by a regularly constituted court, affording all the judicial guarantees which are recognized as indispensable by civilized peoples.

In the context of the law of armed conflicts, violations of the above constitute crimes that are enforceable not only by the parties to the conflict but also by other states party to the law as well as by specially constituted war crimes tribunals such as those for the former Yugoslavia and Rwanda and, since its creation, by the International Criminal Court. The moral floor set by the law of armed conflicts, then, is more than moral; it is also legal. In this connection it is interesting that reference is made to what is "recognized as indispensable by civilized peoples": The specific reference is to "judicial guarantees," but the phrase might well be regarded as referring to the whole list of protections defined. Above I noted the persistence of the idea that international law imposes the principles of "civilization" on the parties to it; here that idea occurs again as an implicit rationale for the floor for conduct established in the law. What is different here is that while the earlier usage was hegemonic, in that it extended Western principles to the remainder of the world, the usage here assumes that the parties to the law agree on the principles stated by means of the floor for conduct in an armed conflict.

In addition to the developments in international law identified above, the emergence of "the responsibility to protect" idea also reflects the widespread public debate on humanitarian intervention that developed during the 1990s, spurred particularly by widespread outrage over atrocities in the conduct of the wars over the breakup of Yugoslavia and by the Rwandan massacre of 1994. During this debate religious bodies in the United States and elsewhere, even those with a record of opposition to the use of military force, took moral positions deploring the violations of basic human rights in these conflicts and supporting humanitarian intervention by military force aimed at stopping them. A prominent example is provided by the statement of the United States Catholic bishops, *The Harvest of Justice Is Sown in Peace*,[5] published in 1993, which devoted significant discussion to humanitarian intervention, explicitly linking the justification of the use of military force to the protection of basic human rights (section II.E.4). (Major American Protestant bodies also supported such intervention during this period.) Central to the bishops' argument was a reference to Pope John Paul II as "outspoken in urging that humanitarian intervention be obligatory where the survival of populations and entire ethnic groups is severely compromised." The bishops continued by observing that the pope had "judged this a duty for nations and the international community." While the bishops' statement continued by cautioning that "nonmilitary forms of intervention should take priority over those requiring the use of force," it also allowed that "military intervention may sometimes be justified to ensure that starving children can be fed or that whole populations will not be slaughtered." While this was a statement by a national conference of bishops, the use of papal language to ground the position taken served to make the point that this was intended to be a statement of principles applying to the world at large, not just to policies and actions of the United States.

The pope's position as described here recalls the language of the Genocide Convention as to the evils to be remedied, but it goes beyond the convention in calling for humanitarian intervention for this reason to be "obligatory," "a duty for nations and the international community." The language of the bishops themselves described only the most basic human rights as those whose violation "may sometimes" justify military intervention. Given the development of human rights law since 1948, it is striking that here it is only the violation of such basic human rights that is presented as offering justification for intervention in response. This reflects, I would judge, the lack of substantial consensus in the international community as to other rights and whether they might deserve similar protection. It also reflects the bishops' formal position that the resort to armed force is inherently morally problematic. What captured attention in such statements as this was that the United States Catholic bishops could accept the use of military force in this kind of case, when they were on record as espousing a "presumption against war" (broadened earlier into a "presumption against the use of force" in the statement published in 1993). But that they extended protection by intervention only to human rights of the most basic sort, rights earlier identified with genocide, is also striking.

It is also doubtful that the United States Catholic bishops, or the Protestant bodies that took similar positions during this period, recognized that what they were advocating in accepting the use of military force in the kinds of cases noted could be regarded as a violation of the prohibition set down in Article 2 of the United Nations Charter against the use of such force except in response to "armed attack." Because of this provision, the armed forces of the country subjected to the intervention called for could reasonably justify armed opposition to the intervention as an aggression to be defended against. That is, such intervention, though for humanitarian purposes, could legally be regarded as an act of aggression against the state in question.

What this debate about humanitarian intervention did, then, perhaps more clearly than the developments in international law itself, was to raise to view the dilemma posed in the state of the law of the time: on the one hand, a body of international agreements of various sorts and levels of authority seeking to identify human rights and provide for their protection against violation; on the other hand, a prohibition against the use of armed force by states except in defense against "armed attack," which had been a principle of international law since the adoption of the United Nations Charter in 1945.

The development of the idea of "the responsibility to protect" took place against this background.

Defining "The Responsibility to Protect"

Besides spurring the public debate over humanitarian intervention, the crises of the 1990s also produced a reaction directly bearing on international law: the formation of the ad hoc International Commission on Intervention and State Sovereignty (ICISS) and its work, whose conclusions were published in 2001 in the form of a report titled *The Responsibility to Protect*.[6] This report and its effect, including especially the idea of "the responsibility to protect" itself and is definition, have generated a great deal of scholarly commentary and international response. Though the present discussion draws on this commentary and sketches important elements in the international response, the aim here is limited to the specific matter of the implications of the idea of "the responsibility to protect" for the conception of sovereignty: How well does it fit with the idea of sovereignty defined in terms of territorial inviolability against interference from outside, and to what degree does it restore the norm that the exercise of sovereignty requires governments to seek the common good of their societies?

While the ICISS report began by affirming that states bear the primary responsibility for protecting the human rights of their citizens, the occasion for the work of the ICISS was, after all, the fact of a serious failure to exercise this responsibility in a number of crises. Accordingly, the meat of the report had to do with what should be done in cases in which states fail in this responsibility, and a major focus of the answer provided by the report was to lay out conditions for military intervention. The framing of these conditions began with a list of "principles for military intervention," which is easily recognizable by persons familiar with the just war idea since it is organized as an interpretation of the categories of just war (though there is no mention of the just war idea as such). It cited, first among these principles, "the just cause threshold," defined as existing under either of two circumstances:

> A. large scale loss of life, actual or apprehended, with genocidal intent or not, which is the product either of deliberate state action, or state neglect and inability to act, or a failed state situation; or
>
> B. large scale "ethnic cleansing," actual or apprehended, whether carried out by killing, forced expulsion, acts of terror or rape.

The principles continued by specifying that the intention of such intervention "must be to halt or avert human suffering," that the intervention is justified only when every nonmilitary option for resolving the crisis has been explored, that the intervention "should be the minimum necessary to secure the defined human protection objective," and that it must offer "a reasonable chance of success" in securing the justifying objective.[7]

Numerous articles and books by international lawyers and international relations specialists have since examined and analyzed in significant detail the ideas put forward in *The Responsibility to Protect.*[8] Though ICISS was neither a governmental body nor one operating under the agency of the United Nations, *R2P* (or "RtoP," as in the articles cited above), as the report quickly became known in shorthand, was subsequently adopted into United Nations usage, being affirmed unanimously, if in a somewhat modified form, at the World Summit Conference in 2005 and reaffirmed by Security Council resolutions, though exactly what it implies, authorizes, and requires remains to be debated and decided in the context of every crisis in which it is invoked. To understand the current status of the still ongoing debate over humanitarian intervention by military force, which also extends to the ethical implications of religious reflection on such possible uses of force, it is necessary to acknowledge the presence of *R2P*, even if in present status its meaning is more limited than in the original form, still somewhat unclear in detail, and interpreted differently by different states as applying to their rights, responsibilities, and obligations in the international sphere, when faced with serious behavior of the sort identified with *R2P*'s "just cause threshold." What is defined by *R2P* as to be protected reflects what is clearly considered a broad consensus as to fundamental rights possessed by all persons. In this sense *R2P* denies a tension between the development of human rights law and the prohibition of "armed attack" across a national border. Under the specific circumstances defined by *R2P*, military action to stop and seek to remedy the particular kinds of serious violations of rights named is presented as not to be construed as constituting "armed attack," that is, military aggression that may be defended against.

The ICISS report thus seeks to reconcile the conception of sovereignty based on the Westphalian system and its included norm of nonintervention with the ICISS's own conception of sovereignty as implying a national and international "responsibility to protect" basic human rights by arguing that the latter is the result of each state's voluntarily joining the United Nations "as a responsible member of the community of nations."[9] The report argues that this does not do away with the Westphalian norm "but is a way of saying that the more traditional notion of state sovereignty should be able to embrace the goal of greater self-empowerment and freedom for people, both individually and collectively."[10] The result, argues the report, is not a "transfer or dilution of state sovereignty" but rather "a necessary re-characterization."[11]

Well, perhaps. This "re-characterization" of state sovereignty is a noble statement of *lex ferenda* (what should be the law) but hardly an accurate description of the reality of the world as it is. States, whether well governed or ruled by tyrants or predators, have a real interest in being secure inside their own borders, and the core element in the Westphalian definition of sovereignty, namely, the sanctity of territorial borders, establishes a powerful protection of that security. Indeed, as we have seen, this idea of sovereignty is based on the idea that there is a fundamental human right of self-defense against attack, whatever the reason offered for the attack. To speak of sovereignty, defined as the right of all states to be secure in their own borders, simply as "the norm of nonintervention" refers only to one implication of that conception of sovereignty, but it is a core element. The ICISS report seeks to find a way to justify abrogating the norm of nonintervention for specific sorts of cases of bad rule: when the ruling authorities engage in acts that directly produce "large scale loss of life" or "ethnic cleansing" or fail to prevent such acts by others, either by inaction or by inability to do so. But the justifying language employed by the ICISS speaks of a more general shift in the relationship of state sovereignty to international order, and this may be a bridge too far in the framing of international law. Well-governed states have no real reason to delegate to the Security Council decisions about their actions that might provide a pretext for some loss of national security. In the case of the badly governed states that the ICISS report aims specifically to target, the motivation is even less: Why should the rulers of such states, whose own actions proceed from their effort to favor one portion of their population at the expense of others, to absolutize their power over the whole society, or to accumulate personal riches at the expense of national welfare, regard United Nations membership as in any way opening the door to interference by other states in what they do? The result, after all, at the minimum may be the loss of some of their power and its benefits, and beyond this they and their close associates may be taken into custody and tried for violating international law.

The ICISS report specifically links its new (or "re-characterized") conception of sovereignty to the conception of human rights laid out in the declaration of 1948 and the covenants on human rights of 1966. Regarding this argument, I would recall two points I have already made.

First, the conception of human rights offered here is by no means the comprehensive seamless garment the ICISS report represents it as being.

Serious differences of perspective and understanding of purpose lie behind each of the agreements cited, as well as the other international statements on human rights that make up the whole body of international efforts to define human rights. Within the United Nations structure, such differences tend to come out in the form of political differences within the United Nations Commission on Human Rights and in the Security Council. In these contexts, consistent agreement and adherence to a common ideal are a chimera; decisions and actions in particular cases are ruled instead by political considerations. This provides only a shaky foundation for weakening the rule of nonintervention in the internal affairs of states.

Second, there remains a serious tension between the idea of justified humanitarian intervention and the norm of territorial inviolability. The ICISS report's "re-characterization" of sovereignty does not remove this tension, though it suggests that the established norm is in fact not absolute and can be overruled if circumstances warrant. This is in fact already the case in connection with the allowance, in Chapter VII of the United Nations Charter, that the Security Council can authorize the use of force across national borders when international peace and security are threatened. But so far as the state use of armed force is concerned, the older norm remains. Also, it is not at all clear that all cases of behavior of the form singled out in the ICISS report as justifying intervention also qualify as threats to international peace and security. So the ICISS report left substantial work to be done.

Adopting and Shaping the Doctrine

The doctrine of "the responsibility to protect," as framed by the ICISS report, received a mixed international reaction. While a number of states, led by Canada, Germany, and the United Kingdom, reacted favorably to the report, the Non-Aligned Movement rejected it. India, one of the states in this movement, argued that the Security Council already had sufficient power to act in humanitarian crises, while Malaysia argued that humanitarian intervention as defined by the ICISS was contrary to international law. China had opposed the ICISS project from the beginning and responded to the report with the position that, while "massive humanitarian" crises were "the legitimate concern of the international community," all questions related to the international uses of force were already the proper concern of the Security Council. Russia took a similar position. The United States rejected the effort in the ICISS report to define criteria for humanitarian intervention, refusing to bind its actions by such criteria and to give precommitments for military action in cases in which the United States had no national interests.[12]

Despite this mixed reaction to the ICISS report, the basic idea that serious and systematic violations of basic human rights could justify military action to stop them and remedy them remained firmly on the table. In 2002 the Constitutive Act of the African Union established "the right of the Union to intervene in a Member State pursuant to a decision of [its] Assembly in respect of grave circumstances, namely war crimes, genocide and crimes against humanity"; in 2003 this list of causes was amended to include other "serious threats to legitimate order."[13] The possibility of intervention by a regional organization as defined here essentially mirrored NATO's decision to intervene in the Kosovo crisis a few years earlier in spite of not having a mandate to do so from the Security Council. As for intervention by an individual state, though the United States had reacted negatively to the ICISS report's laying out of criteria for international action to deal with serious human rights abuses and locating of the authority for such action in the Security Council, in late 2002 and early 2003 United States President George W. Bush gave the "extremely grave violations of human rights" and the "all-pervasive" repression of its own people by the Iraqi regime under Saddam Hussein as one of three justifications for the US use of military force to remove that regime. Bush stated these justifications (the other two were to respond to Iraq's systematic and continuing violation of the terms of the cease-fire that concluded the Gulf War of 1990–91 and related Security Council resolutions and to preempt the likely use of weapons of mass destruction by Iraq) on three occasions: in a speech to the United Nations in September 2002, in his State of the Union speech in January 2003, and in his brief address at the start of the invasion of Iraq a few weeks later. The humanitarian intervention justification never gained traction, however, either in the United Nations or in the US debate, where it was opposed by the military at high levels and never picked up in the religious and ethical debate.

Within the environment of the United Nations, the ICISS report was strongly favored by then Secretary General Kofi Annan, and in 2004 the report of the High-Level Panel on Threats, Challenges and Change endorsed the enforcement by the Security Council of the "emerging norm that there is a responsibility to protect," also affirming and adding to the ICISS report's listing of just cause thresholds and precautionary principles as guides for Security Council action on such matters.[14]

A rather different direction was taken in the Outcome document of the World Summit meeting in 2005,[15] which in two paragraphs (138 and 139) specifically on the responsibility to protect significantly refocused the meaning of this idea away from the question of humanitarian intervention. Rather, such protection is described as a responsibility of "each individual state," with the role of the international community being to support the states in this. Paragraph 138 reads in full: "138. Each individual State has the responsibility to protect its populations from genocide, war crimes, ethnic cleansing and crimes against humanity. This responsibility entails the prevention of such crimes, including their incitement, through appropriate and necessary means. We accept that responsibility and will act in accordance with it. The international community should, as appropriate, encourage and help States to exercise this responsibility and support the United Nations in establishing an early warning capability." Exactly what the nature should be of the support given by the international community through the United Nations is spelled out more fully in Paragraph 139. This paragraph begins by citing this support in terms of the "responsibility to use appropriate diplomatic, humanitarian and other peaceful means, in accordance with Chapters VI and VIII of the Charter, to help protect populations" from the types of harm named in the previous paragraph. Only then does it turn to the possibility of "collective action, in a timely and decisive manner, through the Security Council, in accordance with the Charter, including Chapter VII, on a case-by-case basis and in cooperation with relevant regional organizations as appropriate, should peaceful means be inadequate and national authorities manifestly fail to protect their populations [from the named forms of harm]." Paragraph 139 concludes by expressing mutual commitment to "helping States build their capacity to protect their populations" from such harm.

Again, this represents a significant refocusing away from the earlier emphasis on humanitarian intervention by military force in cases of the kinds of oppression identified. The possibility of such intervention remains, but here it is decoupled from the responsibility to protect itself (which is identified as a responsibility possessed by each state) and expressly subordinated to peaceful efforts by the international community to support states in exercising such responsibility. So far as humanitarian intervention is alluded to (the term itself is not used here), it is by reference to the Security Council's power under Chapter VII of the charter (which has to do with "Actions with Respect to Threats to the Peace, Breaches of the Peace, and Acts of Aggression"), a power that the council had had from the moment it was created. Simon Chesterman's assessment of the result is even more critical: that "the normative content [of the responsibility to protect idea] had been emasculated to the point where it essentially provided that the Security Council could authorize, on a case-by-case basis, things that it had been authorizing for more than a decade."[16] The possibility that individual states (as in the case of Tanzania's intervention in Uganda in the face of Idi Amin's depradations, Vietnam's against Pol Pot in Cambodia, and others) or regional organizations (as in the case of the African Union Constitutive Act or the NATO action in Kosovo) might have their own responsibility to protect persons whose human rights were being seriously and systematically violated in a particular state is not recognized here.

Exactly what this refocused version of the idea of a responsibility to protect means remains somewhat unsettled. At one interpretive extreme, it returns the matter to where it stood before the ICISS report: Such protection is a matter for individual states. This extreme may go too far, since the World Summit Outcome document at least expresses the principle that every state has the responsibility to protect its population from the kinds of harm named. But the older problem—that the governments of states had been in many cases the worst offenders—is sidestepped here. At the other interpretive extreme, the use of military force as a response to a state's failure to protect its population from the kinds of harm named is specifically related in the Outcome document to the Security Council's powers under Chapter VII, and in principle this represents a substantive expansion of the meaning of that chapter and the Security Council's powers under it. Bellamy, whom I have cited above, argues that the agreement expressed in the statement of 2005 was reached "not by the power of humanitarian argument but by bargaining away key tenets of the ICISS's recommendations."[17] But elsewhere Bellamy examines several crises since 2005 in which he believes the responsibility to protect idea was used (none of which involved military intervention) and finds that it was employed effectively, in the form defined by the Outcome document of 2005, in one of these: Kenya after its disputed election in 2007.[18]

Edward C. Luck comments of this, "the ability of RtoP to deliver has been (and will continue to be) mixed." But, he goes on, "it is a bit early in RtoP's young life to judge what it will be when it grows up as a mature policy tool."[19]

The Security Council's authorization to NATO to use force to protect civilians during the armed uprising against the Qaddafi government in Libya provides the only example as of this writing of a clear use of the responsibility to protect doctrine as defined in the Outcome document to justify military intervention for humanitarian purposes. For the purposes of this book, this is especially important, because such use of force exemplifies the clear tension between the idea of sovereignty as territorial inviolability and the idea of sovereignty as involving a responsibility to protect the basic rights of the population of the affected state. The interventionary use of force in Libya took place not only without the approval of the Libyan government but, arguably, in opposition to it, since, while the end of regime change was not part of the formal authorization, the NATO air attacks rather quickly developed as de facto air support for the rebellion's aim of ousting Qaddafi and his regime. Indeed, it is not at all clear that the intervention could have succeeded in its authorized aim without the end of removing the regime responsible for the intended harm of civilians. At the same time, the regime could not realistically have been expected to change its behavior, since doing so would have effectively the same results as its removal: leaving the rulers without authority and power, dead at worst, and subject to international war crimes proceedings if still alive. All the incentives for a predator regime are for it to resist intervention and seek by any means to stay in power; all the incentives for intervention point toward regime change. This underscores the challenge such intervention poses to the idea of sovereignty defined in terms of territorial inviolability. At this writing, the same problems are being played out, with thus far different results, on a larger scale in Syria, where diplomatic efforts to secure protection for the civilian population have so far failed, but without triggering the option of a Security Council decision for military intervention aimed at such protection. In both of these cases, then, the idea of the responsibility to protect has been invoked, though with different results in terms of a military intervention that would implicitly pose a challenge to the established idea of sovereignty. Looking back at the beginnings of the idea of the responsibility to protect, Simon Chesterman has suggested that its significance "was never, in a strict sense, legal. Rather, it was political—and importantly, *rhetorical*."[20] That judgment would still seem to apply well to the current state of the idea.

A broader perspective on the implications of all this for the idea of sovereignty can be gained by a consideration of the idea of humanitarian intervention in itself. Even before the work of ICISS, a responsibility for nations and the international community to act, by military force if necessary, to stop especially outrageous violations of basic human rights was being asserted in the debates centered on such violations in Bosnia, Rwanda, and Kosovo. The adjective "humanitarian" was employed to differentiate military intervention for such a purpose from other forms of intervention, understood as undertaken with motives of national interest of some sort. Because humanitarian intervention, on this conception, was to be undertaken with the altruistic purpose of protecting populations from violations of basic human rights, it could be argued that such intervention did not violate the prohibition of the resort to armed force as set out in Article 2(4) of the United Nations Charter. This is not, though, a convincing distinction. Michael Walzer, considering the idea of humanitarian intervention in 1977, wrote that he had not found any cases of intervention for purely humanitarian reasons, "but only mixed cases where the humanitarian motive is one among several."[21] The same holds for the cases of the 1990s. Especially among the European members of NATO, support for the use of military force in Bosnia and later in Kosovo was tied to the proximity of the conflicts and fear that the consequences would spill over into the rest of Europe unless stopped. High members of the US military establishment cited a lack of national interest reasons in opposing the use of US forces in the Bosnian Implementation Force (IFOR) after the conclusion of the Dayton Accords, and in the United States the lack of a clear national interest reason worked against intervention in the Rwandan massacre of 1994. The cases of Libya and Syria do not, frankly, look much different. In the former case the European members of NATO, which took the lead roles in the military action, had clear national interest reasons for doing so, including opposition to the Qaddafi regime, a desire to have an influence on the rebels, and a show of solidarity with the Arab and African states who wanted an end to the Qaddafi regime. That the United States took only a supporting role in this action also reflected national interest calculations. In the case of Syria, similar kinds of reasoning as in the cases of Libya, Kosovo, and Bosnia apply to the supporters of military intervention against the Assad regime, while Russia's opposition to such intervention reflects its history of military, economic, and diplomatic ties to Syria, fear for Russian citizens living in Syria, and concern that Syrian Orthodox Christians would be at risk should the Assad government fall. Other examples could be cited of the presence of national interest reasoning both in favor of humanitarian intervention and against it.

It is far from clear, in any event, that such reasoning should be discounted as a moral consideration when humanitarian intervention is the issue. The use of military force always comes at a cost to the society that uses it; the use of such force for humanitarian intervention is no different. It also always carries a cost to the society in which intervention is made, including collateral damages to the very people whose protection provides the humanitarian purpose of the intervention. The aim of minimizing such costs—or not incurring them at all—represents moral obligations as well as legal and political ones. In every case in which humanitarian intervention appears as a moral obligation, it should properly be balanced against these other two obligations. National interest, understood as an expression of the obligation of a government to its own society, is thus a proper element in the overall moral consideration and decision. Every empirical case is different, and the balance between these different obligations should be expected to be different in every case as well. To amplify Chesterman's judgment, it is morally important for the conception of sovereignty to identify as a norm for states as well as the international community the responsibility to protect populations from violations to their basic human rights. But what this implies for the future of the idea of sovereignty defined as territorial inviolability or for national interest reasoning in international relations remains to settle out.

What this idea means for individual states is, though, perhaps of more importance than what it implies for the international legal order. Paragraph 138 of the World Summit Outcome document of 2005 places on each individual state the responsibility to protect its population from four especially egregious kinds of harm: genocide, war crimes, ethnic cleansing, and crimes against humanity. This is narrower language than is typically found in the moral debate, where the problem is regularly phrased in the broader terms of especially serious and systematic violations of basic human rights. Even that is a narrower phrasing of the responsibility of government than is found in the older definition of sovereignty as responsibility for the common good. For the World Summit Outcome document of 2005, if a state does not live up to its responsibility as described, it ultimately may be the object of a military intervention to deal with the problem. Thus the state's sovereignty defined as the inviolability of its territory from outside attack is forfeited, at least until the intervention is completed and the forces withdrawn. But so far as the government in that state is concerned, the government that occasioned such intervention by its failure to protect its population against the cited kinds of harm will likely have been deposed in the course of the intervention. So one might argue that assigning each state the responsibility to protect its population against the named kinds of harm shifts the focus of the meaning of sovereignty to the way government is exercised and away from the inviolability of the state's territory from incursions by armed force from outside. This is quite a significant change. So far as this is the case, though, it sets a low bar for the idea of the exercise of sovereignty as responsibility for a state's populace. As a legal definition preparatory to a statement of the right of the international community to intervene to correct the harm being done, such a minimal statement of the nature of the state's responsibility reflects the continuing importance of the territorial conception of sovereignty, even as it provides for a temporary vacation from that norm in the sorts of cases cited. But as a moral definition of the responsibility of governments to their people, it leaves the door open to all sorts of oppression that do not amount to genocide, war crimes, ethnic cleansing, or crimes against humanity. An international community comprising states that meet only the Outcome document's definition of their responsibility to their populations is not much of a moral community. And thus the basic problem with the modern definition of sovereignty remains: Intended as a way to reduce war justified by appeal to higher moral standards, it has no real place for the idea that the right of sovereignty depends ultimately on the government's exercise of a responsibility for the common good of the society governed.

Notes

1. Text at www.icrc.org/hl.nsf/full/390.
2. Text at www2.ohchr.org/english/law/genocide.htm.
3. Text at www.un.org/en/documents/udhr.
4. Text at www.icrc.org/hl/nsf.

5. Text at http://old.usccb.org/sdwp/harvest.shtml.
6. International Commission on Intervention and State Sovereignty (ICISS), *The Responsibility to Protect.*
7. ICISS, *The Responsibility to Protect*, xii.
8. Of particular interest for ethical reflection is the series of articles published beginning in 2005 in the journal *Ethics & International Affairs*; see Bellamy, "Whither the Responsibility to Protect? Humanitarian Intervention and the 2005 World Summit," 143–69; Bellamy, "The Responsibility to Protect—Five Years On," 143–69; Bellamy et al. "Libya and the Responsibility to Protect: The Exception and the Norm," 263–69; Buchanan and Keohane, "Precommitment Regimes for Intervention: Supplementing the Security Council," 41–63; Luck, "The Responsibility to Protect: Growing Pains or Early Promise?," 349–65; Welsh, "Implementing the 'Responsibility to Protect': Where Expectations Meet Reality," 415–30.
9. ICISS, *The Responsibility to Protect*, paragraph 2:14.
10. Ibid., paragraph 2:13.
11. Ibid., paragraph 2:14.
12. On the above and other reactions, see further Bellamy, "Whither the Responsibility to Protect?," 151–53.
13. Ibid., 157.
14. Text at www.un.org/secureworld.
15. http://daccess-dds-ny.un.org/doc/UNDOC/GEN/N.
16. Chesterman, "'Leading from Behind': The Responsibility to Protect, the Obama Doctrine, and Humanitarian Intervention after Libya," 279–85, at 280.
17. Bellamy, "Whither the Responsibility to Protect?," 167.
18. Bellamy, "The Responsibility to Protect—Five Years On," 153–57.
19. Luck, "The Responsibility to Protect," 349–65, at 349.
20. Chesterman, "Leading from Behind," 281, italics in text.
21. Walzer, *Just and Unjust Wars*, 101.

Conclusion

Where do all these investigations leave us? The general answer, I think, is that the current status quo on the matter of sovereignty is somewhat unsettled and that various kinds of work remain to be done to determine how best to move forward from this. I have argued that something of great importance was lost when the older Western conception of sovereignty as responsibility for the common good was replaced at the end of the era of the post-Reformation wars of religion by a new conception defined in terms of the territorial integrity and inviolability of states. But there were good reasons why this happened: The earlier conception of sovereignty was tied to a conception of natural law too closely and inflexibly defined in terms of Western European historical experience and religion, a conception that broke down under the pressures of encounters with new civilizations, especially those of the New World, and then especially as a result of the fracturing of Western European Christianity in the era of the Reformation. These kinds of pressures were new to Western civilization, and it lacked the intellectual and institutional tools to refer to a higher, more universal conception of moral norms that might be able to endure despite religious and other cultural differences. The immediate response to these pressures was negative, as the conception of sovereignty as responsibility for the common good was employed to justify internecine war over contrary religion in Europe and the destruction of indigenous cultures and civilizations in the New World. For the understanding of sovereignty, the developments in Europe had far greater impact than those in the New World, since the savagery of the Reformation-era wars of religion proved a powerful stimulus to different ways of thinking about the nature of political communities and life in such communities.

These different ways of thinking reached for a new conception of what values are common across communities divided from one another by serious religious and other cultural and civilizational differences, and the conclusion ultimately reached was far narrower than the older idea of a common good to be served by political community. The new idea of what is common was the right of each individual person to self-defense against attack from another, and the conception of political order was recast on the basis of this idea, so that ruling authorities, who under the older conception of sovereignty were responsible to the moral order itself for the common good of their societies, were reconceived as possessing political authority only because the people of the society had delegated to them the right to rule so as to exercise as their agent the common right of self-defense. The idea of responsibility for the common good, understood broadly to include the effort to establish justice in all things, here became the much narrower responsibility to provide for the defense of the territory of the political community as a way of defending the people inhabiting that territory. Justice within the community, a major issue in the older conception of sovereignty, was not addressed in this new understanding of political authority. The responsibility of government, understood on the older conception to be a responsibility to the moral order itself, with the ideal of justice established there, thus gave way to a narrower, truncated conception of governmental responsibility as defined by the single common natural right of self-defense.

This new understanding of sovereignty responded well to the immediate crisis in European political life that had taken the form of internecine conflict over religion. The international system that developed after the Peace of Westphalia built on this new understanding; over time it also provided a base for broader internationalist thinking and eventually for the institutionalization of international order through the United Nations. These historical successes argue for the strength of this conception of sovereignty, but it also has had two important negative results: opening the door to predatory actions, including discretionary wars undertaken by states and their rulers with defense as their justification; and protecting rulers who, inside the shield of the territorial inviolability of their states, have used their authority and power to oppress some or all the members of the society they govern. Historically the former problem has received far more attention than the latter: The fear of attack led to the building up of military strength by individual powers and the formation of defensive alliances and the development of balance-of-power politics. While these measures worked to stanch the phenomenon of frequent small wars, they also meant that when wars did erupt, they were larger, more disruptive of ordinary life, and more destructive, as exemplified historically by the two world wars of the twentieth century. The effort to prevent such warfare led to the establishment of international organizations in the forms of the League of Nations and the United Nations and to the adoption of the legal rule of no first use of force by one state against another. These have not, of course, eliminated war, as armed conflict has adapted by taking new forms. I have written elsewhere on the effort to abolish war,[1] and on maintaining moral control in the new forms warfare has taken,[2] but in the present context what is most interesting about these developments in international organization and international law is that, ironically, the nonintervention rule they have established has provided more room for the second problem identified: the use of political authority and power within particular states to oppress some or all members of the population governed. Efforts to address this problem have advanced only with the recession of the fear of major global war after the end of the Cold War. Hidden within this reciprocal relationship is the fact that there is a fundamental tension between the effort to avoid armed conflict involving the uses of armed force across international borders and the desire to avoid the use of governing authority and power to inflict serious oppression within particular states. The development of human rights law and its use in the development of the idea of "the responsibility to protect" have been the response to the existence of such systematic oppression—what in an earlier time would have been called misrule or tyranny. But effective response to such oppression may mean inserting military force into the state in question—humanitarian intervention, in the established phrase—and this looks, prima facie, to be a violation of the rule against initiating the use of force in international disputes. How to resolve this tension?

Putting all this rather more briefly, the conception of sovereignty institutionalized in the Westphalian order and now in the UN system has important faults as well as strengths, though these are different from the faults and strengths of the earlier conception of sovereignty it replaced. On close examination, the strengths of the one tend to counter the faults of the other. Might it be possible to pull them together, producing a combined result that is better than either by itself?

Identifying the different conceptions of sovereignty and their implications has been the focus of the first part of this book, and how to possibly pull them together so as to minimize the faults of each by the strengths of the other has been the focus of the second part. As the discussions of the last two chapters show, I do think there are prospects for doing this, but such a synthesis remains unachieved, and there are real obstacles to it as well.

Chapter 6 shows how the Islamic religion and the culture developed out of it understand the good of the entire community to be the goal of the Islamic state and of legitimate authority over it. This compares directly to the medieval and early modern Western conception of sovereignty in terms of responsibility for the common good and presents the possibility of a revived conception of sovereignty in such terms based on common ground between these two perspectives. So far as a similar understanding of the purpose of political organization and government is also present in the guiding traditions of other cultures, such a revived conception of sovereignty in terms of responsibility for the common good would also be possible with them. But, of course, the problem is that each cultural tradition's understanding of political community and government differs in particular respects from those of other cultural traditions, and when one culture's position is taken as absolute, the possibility of common ground vanishes. For the case of the Islamic religion and culture, I have examined this latter possibility through considering contemporary radical Islamism, and I have suggested this movement needs to be rejected not only by non-Muslims but within the frame of the Islamic religion and culture itself. Even when radicalism is rejected, though, differences across cultural boundaries remain.

My discussion above approaches this matter through consideration of the three kinds of law identified by Georg Schwarzenberger (law based on commonality, law based on hegemony, law based on reciprocal interactions or trade-offs in which the common is maximized while the different is minimized). Focusing on the problem in terms of law fits well into the frame of efforts to think about how international law can be shaped to maximize the areas of agreement about sovereignty as responsibility for the common good across cultural boundaries. But it is important to add that in fact agreements on the implications of fundamental values do not have to be put into the form of law to have real meaning. Functional consensus in particular contexts can serve as well as law or perhaps better, in the specific context, because it is directed to the specifics of the problematic issues in the context in question. One can think of many examples of this kind of phenomenon, from relationships among individuals of different backgrounds all the way to international affairs. A specific example from recent history is provided by the case of the Libyan revolution, where support for armed intervention to protect civilians came from two organizations of Arab states, from within the African Union, and from NATO countries. The consensual agreement among these different groups, and not simply the relevant international law, provided the basis for the Security Council's decision to authorize such intervention. This was a moral consensus as to what needed to be done in the face of the problem presented. In this case, it gave a particular meaning to the existing law. But in other cases—one thinks of the "necessary but illegal" use of force by NATO in Kosovo without Security Council authorization—such moral agreement may justify action beyond what the law specifically allows. Being alert to signs of such functional consensus in specific cases, and indeed maintaining policies aimed at producing such functional consensus, may be a more productive way of thinking about the matter of achieving consensus across cultures than focusing on how to describe common ground in terms of law.

Chapter 7 centers specifically on the matter of the emergent idea of "the responsibility to protect," which as stated in the World Summit Outcome document of 2005 represents a kind of law (not a legal document itself, it expresses agreement on how to interpret the implications of existing law); but as stated in original form in the ICISS report of 2001, it was rather an expression of consensus over a certain moral conception of the responsibility of states and of the international order. The narrowing and truncation of this original expression of "the responsibility to protect" idea in the Outcome document of 2005 suggest the difficulty of translating a moral consensus, however broadly based, into the form of universally binding law. Reaching functional agreement on how to proceed in particular contexts offers a way of closing this gap. It may very well be that the Outcome document's truncated list of cases in which humanitarian intervention may be authorized is the best compromise in law that can be achieved. But the broader idea on which it is based nonetheless remains as a moral consensus, and this moral consensus may coalesce into a functional consensus on appropriate action in specific cases, whatever the floor of the law provides.

In this regard, the Outcome document's explicit affirmation that approval for humanitarian intervention must rest with the UN Security Council may go too far in restricting the right of humanitarian intervention in the face of egregious misconduct by a regime. It was, after all, the Dayton Accords, not Security Council action, that led to a successful form of intervention in Bosnia, and it was NATO, and not the United Nations, that acted to intervene in Kosovo. The failure of the United Nations to prevent the genocidal massacres of Srebrenica and Rwanda, despite the presence of UN peacekeeping forces in both of these places, provides conspicuous reminders of the historical dysfunctionality of the United Nations in regard to the use of military force for humanitarian purposes. Indeed, the structure of the United Nations is such that if it alone is the efficient agent, clear purpose and effective command and control are virtually unimaginable.

In this regard, it may be important to consider further the role of individual states as opposed to the international community, and specifically the Security Council, in regard to serving "the responsibility to protect." The supplementary volume to *The Responsibility to Protect* provides a survey of the military interventions that took place during the first forty-five years of the existence of the United Nations, noting that humanitarian rationales were offered numerous times, but that these justifications were often abused as "a common feature of state practice."[3] This correlates well with Walzer's observation that when he looked for cases of humanitarian intervention, he found no pure ones. But the ICISS supplementary volume also in the same place lists several important state-on-state interventions in the 1970s (India in East Pakistan at the time of the split with West Pakistan, Tanzania in Idi Amin's Uganda, Vietnam in Pol Pot's Cambodia) in which the justifying rationale offered by the intervening states was self-defense, though a humanitarian rationale would have been appropriate, and these interventions all resulted in ending egregious humanitarian abuses. The supplementary volume concludes that these cases "challenge the conventional wisdom that disinterested, multilateral humanitarian interventions necessarily produce greater benefits to populations in distress than ones that are self-interested and undertaken by a state acting alone."[4] One might add the recent armed intervention by French forces in Mali to this list from the 1970s: Though this was a case of "intervention by invitation" to assist Mali in defending itself against forces of al-Qaeda in the Western Maghreb, it also had obvious humanitarian results. I would add a point I have made in discussing humanitarian intervention in other contexts: That whether acting singly or in consort with other states, whether under UN authorization or not, a state in using military force always confronts several sorts of obligations that tend to pull in different directions—obligations to the international order and to the state and its people who are the object of intervention, as well as obligations to its own society, which must bear the cost of the action in lives and treasure. That the three interventions cited from the 1970s (and the recent intervention by the French in Mali) all proceeded under the justification of self-defense may be more than a reflection of the UN Charter's effort to limit the use of armed force by individual states to cases of self-defense; it can also be understood as a recognition by the governments of the intervening states that in their actions they have obligations to the international order as currently constituted and to their own societies, and not just to the people who were the objects of humanitarian abuse in the states that were the objects of these interventions.

Asking about the role of individual states in relation to the international community and, more specifically, the Security Council draws attention to a broader issue in contemporary international affairs, where the nature of states varies enormously, their capabilities to act individually or in ad hoc alliances vary similarly, and their formal and informal roles within the current international system differ in major ways. The category of sovereignty, however defined, in any case refers to states and not to the international community: Groupings of states, up to and including the United Nations and even the Security Council, do not have sovereignty except through the member states. This has implications both for obligations to act in times of crisis and for limits on action. To think of individual states as having responsibilities for the welfare of their populations—as the older conception of sovereignty as responsibility for the common good and the first aspect of "the responsibility to protect" defined by the World Summit in 2005 both provide, in their different ways—is important to affirm, even while doing so leaves room for differences among individual states as to how they seek to serve these responsibilities. To define the possibility of using military force to respond to flagrant failures to exercise such responsibility as limited to the international order takes no account of the responsibility and denies the right of well-governed individual states capable of acting alone or in regional groups to deal with such failures. A proper balance between the two conceptions of sovereignty we have been discussing needs to allow for such action by individual states and groupings of states apart from the international order as a whole.[5]

Finally, I note that the effort to protect states by seeking to prevent recourse to force between states (occasioned historically, as noted above, as a reaction to one of the problems that resulted from the Westphalian system and the conception of sovereignty in terms of territorial integrity) leaves the matter of justice out of the picture. How to understand the meaning of justice is, to be sure, complicated in a context of complex international relations involving states of very different sorts and with different cultural backgrounds. But the complexity of the problem is not a sufficient reason simply to shelve it as a concern. As noted above, the effort to ban uses of force between states acting on their own behalf has not always succeeded; it has failed in important instances, and more generally it has helped to occasion the development of new forms of armed conflict that skirt the ban. My own view is that the focus should rather be not on seeking to prevent the use of force as such but on more robustly defining the right to resort to force and controlling how force, once resorted to, is employed. This is, of course, what the just war tradition as a whole is and has always been about: It provides a moral description of how, why, by whom, and to what end force has a role in the exercise of good government and the provision of good political order. In it, sovereignty as responsibility for the common good has a lexical pride of place, as the resort to force is presented as a tool to be used by the sovereign in protecting and preserving the common good. But that common good is defined in terms of reacting to correct injustice to the end of peace. Peace here is not the absence of the use of armed force but the absence of strife that comes into being only when challenges to justice are met and a just political order is maintained. This, in a nutshell, is what the older idea of sovereignty as responsibility for the common good was about. It would be good to recapture this idea and its components in present and future conceptions of right political order, at both the level of individual states and the level of the international system as a whole.

Notes

1. Johnson, *The Quest for Peace*.
2. Johnson, *Can Modern War Be Just?*; Johnson, *Morality and Contemporary Warfare*; Johnson, *Ethics and the Use of Force: Just War in Historical Perspective*.
3. International Commission on State Sovereignty, *The Responsibility to Protect: Research, Bibliography, Background*, 67.

4. Ibid., 68.
5. See further my discussion in Johnson, *Morality and Contemporary Warfare*, 103–17; and in Johnson, "Humanitarian Intervention after Iraq: Just War and International Law Perspectives," 114–26.

Bibliography

Alighieri, Dante. *De monarchia*. Oxford: Clarendon Press, 1916.

Ames, William. *Conscience, with the Power and Cases Thereof*. N.p., 1639.

———. *Medulla Theologiae*. London: Robert Allott, 1630.

Aquinas, Thomas, Saint. *Selected Political Writings*. Edited by A. P. D'Entreves. Oxford: Basil Blackwell, 1965.

———. *Summa theologiae*. www.newadvent.org/summal; accessed March 30, 2013.

———. *Summa theologica*. Vol. 2. New York: Benziger Brothers, 1947.

Augustine, Saint. *Letters*. Vol. 4 (165–203). New York: Fathers of the Church, 1955.

Bellamy, Alex J. "Libya and the Responsibility to Protect: The Exception and the Norm." *Ethics & International Affairs* 25, no. 3 (Fall 2011): 263–69.

———. "The Responsibility to Protect—Five Years On." *Ethics & International Affairs* 24, no. 2 (Summer 1010): 143–69.

———. "Whither the Responsibility to Protect? Humanitarian Intervention and the 2005 World Summit." *Ethics & International Affairs* 20, no. 2 (2006): 143–69.

Bluhm, William T. *Theories of the Political System*. Englewood Cliffs, NJ: Prentice Hall, 1965.

Bodin, Jean. *On Sovereignty*. Cambridge: Cambridge University Press, 1992.

Born, Lester K. The *Education of a Christian Prince by Desiderius Erasmus*. New York: Octagon Books, 1973.

Buchanan, Allen, and Robert O. Keohane. "Precommitment Regimes for Intervention: Supplementing the Security Council." *Ethics & International Affairs* 25, no. 1 (Spring 2011): 41–63.

Butterworth, Charles. "Al-Farabi's Statecraft: War and the Well-Ordered Regime." In *Cross, Crescent, and Sword*, edited by James Turner Johnson and John Kelsay, 79–100. New York: Greenwood Press, 1990.

Calvin, John. *Institutes of the Christian Religion*. 2 vols. Grand Rapids, MI: Wm. B. Eerdmans, 1957.

Carlson, John D., and Erik C. Owens, eds. *The Sacred and the Sovereign*. Washington, DC: Georgetown University Press, 2003.

Chesterman, Simon. "'Leading from Behind': The Responsibility to Protect, the Obama Doctrine, and Humanitarian Intervention after Libya." *Ethics & International Affairs* 25, no. 3 (Fall 2011): 279–85.

Contamine, Philippe. *War in the Middle Ages*. Oxford: Basil Blackwell, 1984.

Convention on the Prevention and Punishment of the Crime of Genocide. www2.ohchr.org/english/law/genocide.htm; accessed August 15, 2012.

Dawson, Christopher. *Religion and the Rise of Western Culture*. Garden City, NY: Image Books, 1958.

Elshtain, Jean Bethke. *Sovereignty: God, State, and Self*. New York: Basic Books, 2008.

Elton, G. R. *Renaissance and Reformation, 1300–1648*. 2nd ed. New York: Macmillan; London: Collier-Macmillan, 1968.

Ferguson, Niall. *Civilization: The West and the Rest*. New York: Penguin, 2011.

Fukuyama, Francis. *The Origins of Political Order*. New York: Farrar, Straus and Giroux, 2011.

Gewirth, Alan. *Marsilius of Padua: The Defender of Peace*. 2 vols. New York: Columbia University Press, 1951, 1956.

Gierke, Otto. *Natural Law and the Theory of Society*. Cambridge: Cambridge University Press, 1958.

Grotius, Hugo. *The Law of War and Peace*. Roslyn, NY: Walter J. Black, 1949.

Hamilton, Bernice. *Political Thought in Sixteenth-Century Spain*. Oxford: Clarendon Press, 1963.

Hearnshaw, F. J. C., ed. *The Social and Political Ideas of Some Great Mediaeval Thinkers*. New York: Barnes & Noble, 1923.

__________, ed. *The Social and Political Ideas of Some Great Thinkers of the Renaissance and the Reformation*. London: George C. Harrap, 1925.

Huizinga, J. *The Waning of the Middle Ages*. New York: St. Martin's Press, 1924.

Huntington, Samuel P. "The Clash of Civilizations?" *Foreign Affairs* 72, no. 3 (Summer 1993): 22–49.

Hurd, Ian. "Is Humanitarian Intervention Legal? The Rule of Law in an Incoherent World." *Ethics & International Affairs* 25, no. 3 (Fall 2011): 293–313.

International Commission on Intervention and State Sovereignty. *The Responsibility to Protect*. Ottawa, Canada: International Development Research Centre, 2001.

———. *The Responsibility to Protect: Research, Bibliography, Background*. Ottawa, Canada: International Development Research Centre, 2001.

Jansen, Johannes J. J. G., ed. *The Neglected Duty*. New York: Macmillan; London: Collier-Macmillan, 1986.

Johnson, James Turner. *Can Modern War Be Just?* New Haven, CT: Yale University Press, 1984.

———. *Ethics and the Use of Force: Just War in Historical Perspective*. Farnham, UK: Ashgate, 2011.

———. *The Holy War Idea in Western and Islamic Traditions*. University Park: Pennsylvania State University Press, 1997.

———. "Humanitarian Intervention after Iraq: Just War and International Law Perspectives." *Journal of Military Ethics* 5, no. 2 (2006): 114–27.

———. *Ideology, Reason, and the Limitation of War*. Princeton: Princeton University Press, 1975.

———. *Just War Tradition and the Restraint of War*. Princeton: Princeton University Press, 1981.

———. *Morality and Contemporary Warfare*. New Haven, CT: Yale University Press, 1999.

———. *The Quest for Peace*. Princeton: Princeton University Press, 1987.

Kelsay, John. *Arguing the Just War in Islam*. Cambridge, MA: Harvard University Press, 2007.

———. *Islam and War*. Louisville, KY: Westminster John Knox Press, 1993.

———. "Just War, Jihad, and the Study of Comparative Ethics." *Ethics & International Affairs* 24, no. 3 (2010): 227–38.

Khadduri, Majid. *The Islamic Law of Nations: Shaybani's Siyar*. Baltimore: Johns Hopkins University Press, 1966.

Kuper, Leo. *Genocide*. New Haven, CT: Yale University Press, 1982.

Luck, Edward C. "The Responsibility to Protect: Growing Pains or Early Promise?" *Ethics & International Affairs* 24, no. 4 (Winter 2010): 349–65.

Lugo, Luis E., ed. *Sovereignty at the Crossroads?* Lanham, MD: Rowman & Littlefield Publishers, 1996.

Luther, Martin. *Works*. Vols. 45, 46. Philadelphia: Fortress Press, 1962, 1967.

Lyons, Gene E., and Michael Mastanduno, eds. *Beyond Westphalia?* Baltimore: Johns Hopkins University Press, 1995.

Manschrek, Clyde L. *A History of Christianity*. Vol. 2. Englewood Cliffs, NJ: Prentice Hall, 1964.

Markus, R. A. "Saint Augustine's Views on the 'Just War.'" In *The Church and War*, edited by W. J. Sheils, 1–13. Oxford: Basil Blackwell, 1983.

McDougal, Myres S., and Florentino P. Feliciano. *Law and Minimum World Public Order*. New Haven, CT: Yale University Press, 1961.

Miller, David, et al., eds. *The Blackwell Encyclopedia of Political Thought*. Oxford: Basil Blackwell, 1987.

Myers, Robert J., ed. *Religion and the State*. The Annals of the American Academy of Political and Social Science 483 (January 1986). Beverly Hills: Sage, 1986.

National Conference of Catholic Bishops. *The Challenge of Peace*. Washington, DC: United States Catholic Conference, 1983.

Niebuhr, H. Richard. *The Kingdom of God in America*. New York: Harper & Row, 1959.

Nuremberg Principles. www.icrc.org/hl.nsf/full/390; accessed August 7, 2012.

Pattison, James. "The Ethics of Humanitarian Intervention in Libya." *Ethics & International Affairs* 25, no. 3 (Fall 2011): 271–77.

Philpott, Daniel. *Revolutions in Sovereignty*. Princeton: Princeton University Press, 2001.

Protocols to the 1949 Geneva Conventions. www.icrc.org/hl/nsf; accessed August 7, 2012.

Pufendorff, Samuel Freiherr von. *The Law of Nature and Nations*. 5th ed. London: J. and J. Bonwicke et al., 1749.

Rabkin, Jeremy A. *Law without Nations?* Princeton: Princeton University Press, 2005.

Ramsey, Paul. *Basic Christian Ethics*. New York: Charles Scribner's Sons, 1950.

———. *The Just War*. New York: Charles Scribner's Sons, 1968.

———. *War and the Christian Conscience*. Durham, NC: Duke University Press, 1961.

Reichberg, Gregory M., Henrik Syse, and Endre Begby, eds. *The Ethics of War*. Malden, MA: Blackwell, 2006.

Russell, Frederick H. *The Just War in the Middle Ages*. Cambridge: Cambridge University Press, 1975.

Schwarzenberger, Georg. *The Frontiers of International Law*. London: Stevens and Sons, 1962.

Strayer, Joseph R. *On the Medieval Origins of the Modern State*. Princeton: Princeton University Press, 1998.

Tierney, Brian. "Religious Rights: An Historical Perspective." In *Religious Human Rights in Global Perspective: Religious Perspectives*, edited by John Witte Jr. and Johan D. Van der Vyver, 17–45. The Hague: Martinus Nijhoff, 1996.

United Nations. Report of the High-Level Panel on Threats, Challenges and Change. www.un.org/secureworld; accessed August 9, 2012.

United States Conference of Catholic Bishops. "The Harvest of Justice Is Sown in Peace." 1993. http://old.usccb.org/sdwp/harvest.shtml.

Universal Declaration of Human Rights. www.un.org/en/documents/udhr; accessed August 7, 2012.

Vanderpol, Alfred. *La Doctrine scolastique du droit de guerre*. Paris: A. Pedone, 1919.

Vattel, Emerich de. *The Law of Nations; or Principles of the Law of Nature*. London, 1740.

Walker, Williston. *A History of the Christian Church*. Rev. ed. New York: Charles Scribner's Sons, 1959.

Walzer, Michael. *Just and Unjust Wars*. New York: Basic Books, 1977.

Weber, Cynthia. *Simulating Sovereignty*. Cambridge: Cambridge University Press, 1995.

Weigel, George. *Tranquillitas Ordinis*. Oxford: Oxford University Press, 1987.

Weiss, Thomas G. "RtoP Alive and Well after Libya." *Ethics & International Affairs* 25, no. 3 (Fall 2011): 287–92.

Welsh, Jennifer. "Civilian Protection in Libya: Putting Coercion and Controversy Back into RtoP." *Ethics & International Affairs* 25, no. 3 (Fall 2011): 255–62.

———. "Implementing the 'Responsibility to Protect': Where Expectations Meet Reality." *Ethics & International Affairs* 24, no. 4 (Winter 2010): 415–30.

Wright, Quincy. *A Study of War*. Rev ed. Chicago: University of Chicago Press, 1965.

Wright, Robin. *Sacred Rage: The Crusade of Modern Islam*. New York: Linden Press/Simon & Schuster, 1985.

Index

www.ingramcontent.com/pod-product-compliance
Lightning Source LLC
LaVergne TN
LVHW041110090826
844660LV00056B/83

* 9 7 8 1 6 2 6 1 6 1 0 5 4 *